The Sales Manual

A guide to a career in sales

Dan Doyle

Dedication

This book is dedicated to all the sales warriors who have fought in the trenches, taken the red eyes, put up with unbelievable circumstances, and management year after year in the pursuit of the almighty dollar!

And to my son, I couldn't have done this without you!

Table of Contents

Introduction	1
Do you really want to be in sales?	6
Sales 101	16
The Network	30
The Real Work	35
Presenting the Story	45
Negotiating & Closing	51
The Best Part - Getting Paid	56
Sales Management & Training	61
The Legacy Sales Rep	73
Sales Tools & Process	78
The Cloud	84
AI: Savior or Skynet?	88
The End Or the Beginning	98

Introduction

First of all I need to explain that I am not a writer. I am a sales person and storyteller. Being a storyteller has been a benefit for me in my long career in sales. We will see together if that translates into this business book. The goal of the final product was to provide information that helps with all aspects of sales. From sales, management, training, negotiating, and forecasting it covers a great deal. However, the biggest message in this book is for those people looking to be sellers or increasing their skills in sales. This book is Sales 101 and 201 period. Do you understand the basics of selling? This book will help you decide, if you are willing to do all it takes, to be super successful as a seller. If you are already a professional it can help you make it to the next level. Let's get something straight, this book is not for everyone. I do not hold back on anything!

If you think that sales will be an easy job you should put this book down and look for a different career. This book will take you on what I would call a hard left turn in the idea of sales in business. With all the different sales models out there today, the ideas I will be describing may seem disruptive to some or even old-fashioned to others and it should. What you will find is that these ideas will provide a solid foundation for anyone looking for a career in sales and those looking to transform a sales organization. We will look at three primary ideas and then a few other things to support these ideas within this book. The first is a litmus test for people wanting to get into sales. The second is basic blocking and tackling you will need to do in sales. Last, the goal is to help find an edge, especially in the training and/or expansion of a sales team. This will help those already in sales and managing sales teams. The rest of the book provides common sense perspectives on how to better integrate a company with their sales teams. This will help drive greater revenues and increase employee job satisfaction. While I wrote this mainly to help new sellers I think you will find something in here for everyone in the sales field.

Understand what this book is and what it isn't. This book dives into <u>outside</u> sales. It offers insights into the modern business challenges faced today and aspects of business that directly affect revenues i.e. sales. While not all inclusive, and what single book really can be, the hope is that it opens minds to realize that there are many commonsense theories that many large companies continually miss on. This book is aimed at those in B2B (business to business) sales. While many things in this book cover all aspects of all types of sales it is much more impactful in B2B. Retail, B2P (business to personal), and extreme commodity type sales can get a lot out of this. However, if you're looking for 300 pages of extreme boiler room type of lead generation selling tips or selling your workout routine on Instagram this isn't for you.

You may have noticed that this book is not overly verbose. I've kept this book at this length for a very specific reason. Most busy businesspeople don't have the time to spend reading the "War and Peace"[1] of Sales. Those still in school don't want to waste time wading through another thick textbook. These are the reasons that

---

[1] War and Peace is a Novel by Leo Tolstoy

this book is short, to the point, with a few examples, stories, and zero fluff. I have worked hard on my own work life balance and absolutely would not push anything that would disrupt someone else's ability to do the same!

In today's world, a new company will build a product and then surround that product with the component parts needed for running a business. This is what is taught in many of the business schools. They will get everything assembled, then decide on creating a sales strategy and sales force as one of, if not the last step. Well, I'm here to tell you that this theory is wrong and a new path needs to be taken! A company cannot exist if it cannot sell a product. Why then is it the last thing they think of? Creating a synergistic sales company requires a sales methodology that is integrated from day one. Say you have an idea for a new mousetrap. What you need to do is determine at that very point HOW you will convince the world that your new mousetrap is the best, then build it. Founders usually have the most trouble understanding this because they think EVERYONE will want to buy it "because" it's better. When in reality no one just "wants" it, they must be "Sold" on it. A big competitor in all sales is the "good enough" theory. When a company has something that does the job and is good enough they don't usually look to replace it.

In this arena, you will see a ton of business books on Selling and on how to run a business. A HUGE majority of these books have been written by a specific type of person. You will see a "founder" of a company write a book about their experience creating an amazing company. This is great for reference if you are planning on spinning up a similar type of company, but the view is usually myopic. Chances that you'll have the same type of experience, the same type of people, and processes in what you are doing are extremely slim. You will also see many books come from the "when you can't do, teach crowd". These are theorists, trainers and the educators that have no real experience but love to tell people how they should do things. These are always a hard pass for me as everything they look at is an amalgamation of theories based on parts of other theories or maybe some successful businesses that they've had nothing to do with. Another is the "leader" vision. This is usually a person from a particular company, not necessarily a founder, but someone that has been with the company for an extremely long time. These types push the story of successes built over a long time with one, maybe two companies that they've continued to repeat. What they don't tell you is that often they have been successful in a captured market where they are the majority player and have had repeat customers for YEARS. This is due to long term relationships or just a locked-up market thus never really having to "sell".

When you're doing your research for a direction to take or a guru to follow, you need to examine all these paths and then determine if any of these paths will be successful for YOU and YOUR personality. Maybe though you take the path of one that has taken a different journey. A journey through multiple companies, that participated in multiple different sales processes, selling multiple different products and services over a long time. And one that has always been successful regardless of the product, territory or company. Note the large amount of personal "patting on the back" by the author who is often sarcastic. Broad, cross functional experience matters. Being the "Jack of all trades and master of none is still often better than the master of one"[2] is one of my favorite sayings. If you've only been drawing from experiences from one company, one method, and one north star you are significantly shorting yourself on what can make you better in sales or any other role for that matter.

Each company and each sales strategy must have the ability to mold whatever process that you decide on to its own business process. Don't try and force yourself or your company into a

---

[2] This quote is often attributed to William Shakespeare

strategy for the sake of having a particular strategy if it makes you change your foundations too much. Be flexible and be open to ideas, as you need to be able to improvise, adapt, and overcome for any number of reasons. You can't do that with overly rigid processes. Sticking with a common sense approach allows that flexibility.

Over the years I have read close to 100 books on sales and probably taken 100 classes. Remember I'm in sales, my numbers may be exaggerated. I have listened to every possible version of how to do the exact same thing (sell) over and over. What I have learned through the years is that it's best to just stick with the basics. I have weeded out all the crap that others include to fill page counts (apart from this introduction) so you can get to the meat of the topic and move on to the important information. Hopefully you'll agree in the end!

Ok, enough of the fluff I promised wasn't in here, let's get to it!

CHAPTER 1

Do you really want to be in sales?

This is the big question! Do you think that you really want to be in sales? Do you have 10 pounds of brain damage? Why? Because that's what it takes! Just kidding, kind of, not really. It's understandable that many people are attracted to sales, the allure is very real. You see what appears to be easy hours, you see what appears to be high pay, time for family, and hobbies. What's not to like! This chapter explains much of the minutiae of sales that you may not be aware of. By the way, if it sounds like I'm trying to talk you out of a sales career in a way I am, so I hope you are ready!

I have some harsh reality for you, sales is not always unicorns and rainbows. There is a ton of hard work involved especially when you are just getting started. It is true that it can be a very lucrative career if you can handle the rollercoaster that is sales. Now that I have you all excited about this! Let's chat about what it means and what it takes to be in sales along with the all the little details about the job that you probably haven't thought about. One more quick note, this is directed towards individuals looking at "outside" sales jobs. Much of it will help inside sales as well but this is directed towards the outside sales representative role.

Over the next several pages we'll discuss sales, what it takes, and how to be successful. No BS, no fluff, no overly detailed case studies, just the facts. If you've made it this far you might be asking "who is this guy and why should I spend my time listening to him?". Well, here's a quick bio for you. I have over 30 years of experience in outside sales, look me up on LinkedIn for the detail, call it homework! Your first cold call task! I've worked for small local companies, pre-IPO companies, all the way up to global companies like Cisco, IBM, and Amazon Web Services in sales and sales management roles. I've called on small "mom and pop" accounts all the way up to the largest global service providers like AT&T, and the Department of the Navy. Why did I write this book? I want to share what I've learned so many of you won't have to try and recreate the wheel. So that you don't spin your wheels doing things that just don't work. I'm also tired of watching the corporate machines grind through good people wanting to explore this work as a career and want to help those that have the desire to succeed in sales.

One of the things we need to talk about is the type of person that you need to be in order to be in sales. What you are probably expecting is that I'm going to tell you that you must be tall, good-looking, outgoing, the life of the party, gregarious, and tenacious! Well, almost all of that is wrong! Anyone can be in outside sales as long as you have two things, drive and curiosity. The most important thing though in my humble opinion? You must have a degree of Magnum PI[3] in you, whether that is Tom Selleck or Jay Hernandez, though personally I'm still team Tom. Looks and personality don't hurt but drive and curiosity are still more important. We are a superficial society after all, but most customers

---

[3] Magnum PI is a detective TV Show

couldn't care less about how their sales representatives look. Customers want the people that are selling to them to be responsible, honest, and dependable because parts of their business will depend on your company being able to deliver what you are selling to make them successful.

Being in sales sounds simple right? Make a call, get a meeting, sell some stuff, and get a big check! Well, there are about 9000 steps in there that you're missing. If there weren't everybody would be doing it right? The first thing you need to do is get an actual sales job. Your first one won't necessarily be easy to get or the right one if you don't have the experience. This is when I hear you asking yourself, "how do I get the experience if you won't hire me?". If you're in college and reading this, get yourself into an internship program by junior year. Most of the time you'll have to work for free for a couple months (typical summer internship) and if you're lucky they'll like you and give you that entry level sales opportunity after you graduate. If you are trying to change careers or are not in school, there may still be an internship opportunity out there if you can handle not being paid (no cash or little cash) for a little while. If you can't you're probably going to have to get your experience by working your way into a sales role. What does that mean? Long story short, just find a place to start doing something sales related or take any sales job available. Sitting around waiting for the "right" opportunity won't get you anywhere.

To give you a better idea of what I mean by this, here is what I did to get started. I didn't start out in sales, never wanted to be in sales and many times I wanted to kick the ass of the person that pulled me into it. I started out as the technical guy, running computer networks, doing technical support, utilizing some of the skills I learned in the Navy. A friend of mine called me because he got a job selling something very technical and he had no background in the technology. He asked me to fill a role as his "system engineer", basically a pre-sales technical support guy. Over a couple years I had the opportunity to move into a direct sales position and moved my way up from there. This brings up a good point on sales career paths. Some people are perfectly happy being a direct salesperson and nothing else. Other people want to get to that management role, whether it's sales manager, regional VP or all the way up to president/CEO. The second is very possible, the current CEO of Cisco (Chuck Robbins) started out in sales and after I think 20 years or so he made it to the CEO's office. (Check his LinkedIn) Now he was a huge outlier. Many will make it to sales manager or director and stop in that middle role, but it is possible to keep going. The thing about moving up into management in sales is that the first step up to sales manager is usually a pay cut and leads to much longer and more stressful hours. However, if you can handle that for a couple of years, you can make it to the level above that and jump back up to higher pay, better work life balance etc. Just something to think about when you get into corporate sales. I did the management thing a couple times but decided after a certain point that I was happy with the money and the work life balance as a salesperson. My path was very similar to many technical people in the IT industry but not everyone gets the opportunity to make that kind of transition. The opportunities are there to change roles within a company once you get established. Just keep your eyes and ears open for the chance.

Back to getting that first job. I've spoken to many people over the years that may worry about applying to a job whose description mentions C-Level relationships. Companies that list job openings for people with experience "selling to C-level/C-Suite" are comical. Most C-suite folks never talk to salespeople unless a dollar value triggers it or the product/solution is that impactful to the company. They have people that do that work for them! And the purchasing department will usually protect that level of executives at all costs. Smaller accounts where an organization is flat may have more access to those titles. Ultimately those senior leaders do have accountability for all the decisions but in the Fortune 500 world, sales at that level rarely happens. You may have the opportunity to create high level relationships, and you should always try to attain executive sponsorship opportunities.

People that have been doing this for a while know that C-level relationships are challenging from an actual business perspective. How much business is the CEO/CFO/CIO going to sign off on? What deals are they going to do versus the people below them making the decisions? While the C-level may have some very strategic visionary plans, your access to them will really be dependent on several factors. Their schedules, their organization structure including how they delegate authority and in general how big the companies are. Saying that you have C-level relationships is great and all, but if you're only seeing them twice a year, the impact on the bottom line of your selling motions really is negligible. Focus on a broader strategy than top down and don't worry about the job description.

Another reality regarding C-level. A discussion that isn't often had is on how many companies are going to allow a sales rep to have those C-level relationships? Many companies will want their own executives to have that relationship or be that touch point. This happens especially when you get into large accounts. We'll talk about executive sponsors a bit later.

My rather lengthy point is don't let a job description scare you from applying for a role. Many times, the description is canned text that HR puts into every one of their job openings. If you don't apply you won't ever get the chance to interview. The often-used quote of "you miss 100% of the shots you don't take" from Wayne Gretzky applies.

Ok now we've shown some paths to sales and you've worked into a role, now what? Most companies will put you through some type of sales training that they have decided for this point in time is their "process". You'll hear things like Challenger, SPIN, or other sales methodologies of the day (the current bright shiny object) that the company wants you to adhere to or at least pretend to adhere to. The reason behind these methodologies is so they can track what and how you are doing in your job. This also drives much of the engine running the rest of the business. They'll give you a good couple of days or maybe a week of this training which will include working in their CRM tool (think salesforce.com). It will also provide some type of quarterly or annual "training goals" that you'll have to meet to stay in the good graces of management. Training will also include background on what you are selling or at least some of what you're selling. Usually this is barely enough for you to get out the door to sell because companies just don't like to invest that much in salespeople. The expectation is that you can sell, regardless of what they give you to sell. They expect you to "study" on your own time and to try and learn from your peers. Regardless of the actual training you'll still be expected to increase your knowledge of the company's products and/or services over time on your own. This is to show that you are competent to represent the company on an ongoing basis. If you're reading this book, you are steps ahead of the rest! Let's say you have managed to get a job; you've been trained so now you must get out there and sell, right? If you're lucky you may get to shadow a more senior salesperson for a few meetings to see how they do their job but don't count on it. Frankly, on-the-job training is the best way to learn sales but most companies don't do that right now.

Let's get back to one of those initial points, make a couple calls and get some meetings! How about making a ton of calls and getting "a" meeting. Cold calling is difficult at best and unfortunately, it's the way most people start out. When you have no contacts at a company you must smile and dial. (Old saying but still accurate). We will get to cold calling shortly. This is one of the primary reasons that more seasoned sales reps are often brought in and paid quite a bit more by large companies as their networks are worth the extra money, in theory. That network is something that you will need to strive to build throughout your career. We'll talk about your network and how to build it shortly as well.

As you continue to determine if you want to be in sales, one of THE biggest questions you need to ask yourself is can you get used to hearing "no" every day? That is one of the biggest hurdles in sales. You are constantly "asking" for the meeting or the sale and you are constantly told "no". You must develop thick skin because "no" comes in many forms and some are just not nice. At times you will be in heated discussions with your customer trying to close a deal and you will be told "no" for reasons that have nothing to do with you or your sales ability. It may be a financial decision; it may be a relationship decision (see build your network). It may even be something as simple as the customer believes they've been buying too much from you and they need to give a deal to someone else just to keep you and your company "in line". (It happens) I know that sucks but remember I'm giving you reality. If your ego can't handle the constant flow of "no" sales is not for you. You'll even see books on negotiating deals that try to teach how to get to yes! The question is, do you think you can handle it?

One of the other big things you must deal with in sales is all of the daily work you have to do. Most salespeople defer doing this work until the last possible moment much like a high schooler with a project that is due. I referenced CRM earlier, that is the customer relationship management tool that all salespeople must get used to as part of their daily life. It's where you (should) have all your contacts stored but you'll keep them in your phone anyway. It's where you create and manage opportunities which turn into quotes and then sales orders. It's also where you and your management will forecast sales for their management. They will then in turn provide details to the operations side of the house so that group can be prepared to order or build products for delivery to your customers. Forecasting is the estimate of how much you think you will sell over a period of time and can be the bane of your existence. Depending on the company they will expect you to have your forecasts updated monthly, weekly or even daily. This is usually dependent on the transactional nature of the business and your management. The higher the transactional rate the more often you will update your forecast. You will then attend sales meetings with your local manager who will grill you on details of said forecast. They will expect you to know absolutely everything about each deal. Management will have you repeat these details to them time and time again until the deal is lost or won because they rarely ever use the CRM tool for what it's meant for. In some situations, you will have the tool updated and then management will send out a spreadsheet to complete because they don't trust the information in the tool! Sometimes it's not as bad as I've led on but I'm trying to prepare you for when it is.

A couple of other things live in the administrative piece of sales including: expenses to cover your mileage, entertainment of customers (if your customers are allowed to be entertained), and mobile phone (if you're lucky). Make sure you understand the expense process in detail. Don't ever leave money on the table that you spend on the company's behalf.

The last big thing you need to be able to deal with in sales is that unsaid phrase that all salespeople have in their heads. Shortly after you've had a great month, quarter or year. Maybe you blew out your number, won a trip to sales club, got the big check and think you're on chill street for a while but you aren't. Another big ego destroyer in this business is that you're only as good as your "next" sale. The phrase that you must learn to live with for the entirety of your career is: "What have you done for me lately!" It's rarely if ever said directly but it is implied always! If someone does say that to you though, start looking for another job. Never stay anywhere that is toxic.

Another topic that we need to cover in sales, whether you're trying to break into sales or moving around to your next role, is the type of company you want to work for. You will need to think about the industries where you may like to work. Do you want to work in IT sales? Do you want to try medical sales? Experiment with your first job(s), if you don't like that industry you can change. Don't feel compelled to stay in any particular industry just because that is where you started. As you grow in your career, always keep your options open.

A big choice in choosing a role is the different sizes of the companies you work for. For example, SMB is the small to midsized business class, the next is what we call commercial size (determined in each industry), and then the Enterprise companies (Think Fortune 500). Each has its own challenges and you may want to try different levels over time to see what you like or where you fit in the best. You may get lucky and the first area will be your goldilocks. SMB territories usually have a large number of accounts. Sometimes you'll hear that you have every account in your state. Depending on the state, that could be a few hundred accounts. This size account has one big challenge, you don't really get the opportunity to develop deep relationships as most of your business will end up being very transactional. It has its benefits once you get a territory up and running as you will get certain level of recurring business or a "run rate". You will usually be asked to add a certain percentage to that run rate to grow your business every year.

Commercial sized accounts can move you into the lower end of the "Fortune" account level. Many will have name recognition but those also come with an increased amount of competition because of that space. Depending on your company you could have up to 50 accounts like this. You will find the 80/20 rule starts to come into play with this sized account and account planning becomes a bigger deal as do relationships. Lastly, you get into the large Enterprise accounts. These accounts, depending on the business relationship, can literally move the stock price of a company based on their purchasing relationship in some situations. You may have only one account of this size but rarely more than a handful as there is just so much information and activity in an account of this size that you won't have time to handle more than a couple.

Account planning in these is key as are long term and cross-company relationships.

One last thought in this section about a sales career. The economy in our beloved country has its ups and downs but even in the most severe downturn companies will always need one thing, salespeople! They are needed even more in down economies. You'll see more marketing dollars and more salespeople added when the economy is bad. This is so that a company has additional paths to revenue and to making its promised numbers. Sure, you'll see the occasional large company have a bad quarter and announce layoffs where sales teams are hit a bit but here's an inside secret, so please don't tell anyone. They do that on purpose to reduce staff in slow areas so they can hire more in areas that are performing well. The areas doing well always need more feet on the street! Yeah, it's a pretty sneaky process and not very nice but it's been going on for years. The upside is that there will always be a need for skilled salespeople.

If you can handle all these challenges, you "MAY" be able to make it in a sales career

CHAPTER 2

Sales 101

Wow that was a lot! If you have made it this far, against my advice, then you have proven that you have questionable judgement and could make it in sales! If you really want to do this let's get started and learn some commonsense methods to get your sales career moving.

If you are EXTREMELY lucky you may walk into a situation where relationships have already been established and you'll just have to work on rebuilding a relationship or two to maintain a book of business. In entry level sales this is highly doubtful. If your company has been around for a while there may have been contact at one point or another with someone inside your targets, but you'll have to vet those out just like a greenfield account. What is greenfield? Greenfield is a net new account or territory where there have been no (or very little) previous sales.

Let's assume for a minute that your territory is greenfield. Before you even attempt to contact your first customer you must do your research, this includes understanding what the companies that you are calling on actually do. Nothing makes a prospective customer angrier than a salesperson coming to sell something when they have no idea what the company even does. For example, don't go into Cisco and try and sell them a better material for wrapping food, they are Cisco not Sysco! (Google it) The question is, where do you start your research? First it should start with internal company knowledge from your coworkers and company sales tools. Then your network, if you have one, but more on networking soon. If you don't have a significant dataset internally or a network, welcome to the world of Google and LinkedIn. I'm sure you've heard of them.

The first step is simple though, finding the website for the company you are working on and then drilling into the details. I suggest taking notes or getting out your highlighter at this point. Websites can be detailed; you will want to hit the about section first and understand the company's executive leadership. These people will become more important as we begin to identify contacts. This section should also include the company goals as well as a mission statement. It's good to know what a company's vision and goals are should it ever come up. From there you'll want to go to the investor relations tab. Here's where many salespeople slack off. You do not need a degree in accounting or economics to gain a massive amount of information about a company from their financial documents! All you need to do is read and take notes. Most of the documents are available as PDF so you can download them too. I highly suggest printing many of these documents out, so that you may more easily highlight or underline areas of interest to what you are trying to target. 10-Ks[4] and 10-Qs[5] have a wealth of underlying information that you can utilize as do the quarterly earnings release statements and presentations. Most public

---

[4] The form presents a financial picture of the company, detailing its revenues, assets, and liabilities for the previous year.

[5] A 10Q is like a 10K but significantly less exhaustive

companies put all this information out there, but private companies usually do not. Private companies may provide that level of future projections but part of being private is not having to do that.

In these documents, public companies will often give detailed information on areas where the company is investing now and in the future. Hidden in accounting line items will be budgets for projects that may provide even more detailed specifics on areas you'll be interested in. You can infer based on an investment now what they may be needing in the future to support these current initiatives. This goes back to your detective abilities. Great salespeople will put the puzzle pieces together to find some hidden business opportunities. Even details on legal matters like lawsuits can help you with sales.

Other sources of company information can be found in the Public Relations section of the company website. Specifically press releases as companies like to brag about the wonderful things that their products and services provide. They will post big wins that they've had and new partnerships. This type of information may affect how you are planning your attack. Read through press releases from the last year, anything older is probably not relevant, and see if you can find anything that could be impactful for you. Wins that they announce may show a need for expansion in some areas, including future hiring. The career section can also provide visibility into new opportunities based on the type of people they are trying to hire. Partnerships will help you determine if you have a growth opportunity due to the partner providing an extra channel of sale for the company, but it also may provide information on a new competition that you may be faced with that is working with that partner. More about partners will be discussed in the networking section.

Press releases around humanitarian or charitable programs provide you with potential areas to partner with your customer on some of their outreach which gives another entry point. These types opportunities can usually be developed once your business relationship is a bit more mature. Showing the customer that you have interest in helping them in this way is a good way to build relationships outside of your targeted areas. Remember you must fully understand a company's business in order to sell to them. This includes factors inside and outside of the customer that may affect sales.

After the company website has been thoroughly investigated with a fine-toothed comb, it is time to head back to Google or Duck-Duck-Go, whichever search engine you prefer. Just do simple searches on the company and you should find both good and bad articles on a company. These fall under the trust but verify condition that I often repeat as you won't necessarily be able to confirm the truth on your first try. This is the internet so unless you find multiple supporting articles assume something is false until otherwise confirmed. LinkedIn also comes into play here as it is the defacto social media for business. You'll find many quotes and comments from various people both inside and outside of a company on this tool. Again, I go to trust but verify because LinkedIn has become as much of a "Look at Me" tool as it is a business tool. You will have to wade through company employees trying to make statements about wonderful things "they" are doing with the company as you will things the company is actually doing. However, you will find good nuggets in there, more on LinkedIn later.

TIP For the public companies, do a search on their stock symbols. Often you will find different articles that can help you with the financial health of a company and explain larger business deals they are working on.

You may be asking yourself at this point, "why should I do all this, it doesn't have anything to do with what I'm selling!". Sorry to tell you, it does. I had similar thoughts when I was starting out and especially when I was in the Navy. In boot camp, we had to do what seemed to be very lame and monotonous tasks like folding our clothes a very specific way so the seams all faced one direction. We also had to make our beds so there were no wrinkles and the corners were all tucked in just right. This was the beginning of the process to teach all of us "attention to detail" and it did just that. These tasks laid the foundation for what came next. Everything I'm suggesting you do will build on this theory of attention to detail and help you sell.

One of your primary goals in sales is to gain trust with your customer. Showing them that you care enough to understand their business more than just superficially is an important part of the process. Documents or data points from your research that you will gather and bookmark will also provide you with valuable information for your account plans that you will build for each customer later. Side note, you should be able to attach or import documents into your CRM tool but if you can't I highly recommend you create folders on your computer to store these documents. I will reference account plans quite a bit, but due to the often massive differences between how companies do them I won't go into detail on them.

TIP As you create a folder for each customer, make sure you date the subfolders so you're able to reference the correct information later.

It is now time to embark upon a time-honored adventure in sales, the bane of existence for some, a joyous exercise for others. You are now entering into the world of cold calling. A task that every salesperson has gone through at one point or another during their careers. Cold calling really should be called investigative sales. You will have to spend an inordinate amount of time trying to figure out whom within a company you need to connect with to make a sale. This builds upon what you read above by gathering more details about your prospective clients.

Seems easy right? I'm sure my new company has a list of all the contacts within my new accounts! Yeah, good luck with that. You may have a few floating around in an old CRM system or spreadsheet, but chances are that it's time for you to become Thomas Magnum. Again you will want to Google the company you are targeting. Just as we discussed previously about gathering data on the company. Go to the home page and just start snooping around. In the about section, as we discussed earlier, you may see a list of senior management types. You should have made some notes of all those people and their roles. You may also find lists of names and titles in the financial information I mentioned that you found on the investor relations web pages.

TIP I suggest setting up a spreadsheet to help you keep track contacts as it will also help you in developing a heat map later. What's a heat map? A heat map helps you keep track of what type of relationship you have with different people in an account. The simple items you should name the fields are name, title, primary phone, mobile phone, and email. You'll also want a comments or notes section to remind you of what your last discussion with each contact was about and when. I will usually use red, yellow and green highlights to remind myself how well I and the company get along with each contact. This will also be important with account planning. See example on the next page. (note the contacts are fictitious)

Sales 101

Account	Contact Name	Title	Email	Office Phone	Mobile Phone	Comments
John Deere	George Clooney	CFO	GFClooney@JD.com	(555) 555-5555	(555) 555-5555	Left msg 6-26
	Brad Pitt	VP Marketing	BWPitt@JD.com	(555) 555-5555	(555) 555-5555	Next Meeting 12-12
	Lance Armstrong	VP Health	LGArm@jd.com	(555) 555-5555	(555) 555-5555	Follow up on MH article
Hallmark	George Washinton	President	GHWash@Hall.com	(555) 555-5555	(555) 555-5555	Call about President's day card
	Abe Lincoln	Artistic Director	ABLinc@Hall.com	(555) 555-5555	(555) 555-5555	No response from previous email exchange. Need followup
Diamond Exch	Limon Zurga	Buyer	LZur@DIA.com	(555) 555-5555	(555) 555-5555	10-2 Left msg about security process Meeting follow-up. Checking with Rusty on
AC Delco	Basher Jones	Engineering	Basjo@ACD.com	(555) 555-5555	(555) 555-5555	vault dimension

You've put together a list of who you think may be your primary contacts started so you're ready to start contacting them right? Wrong. Unless the companies are small, and even in some cases very small, chances are you won't get ahold of these people directly. They have, especially in enterprise or Fortune level accounts, an army of people to keep you away from them. However, now you can start combing through LinkedIn for these senior people and you will start to find not only more details on them, but <u>their</u> networks.

Don't understand why you need to research their network? That you need to only get in touch with the executives? Again you need to think about attention to details. It shouldn't surprise you that often these executives have many contacts <u>within</u> their own organizations that you will want to know about. Employees like to follow the executives in the company they work for to make sure that they keep up to date on some things they may not be privy to in their day-to-day jobs. It is also a means of brown nosing to kiss up to the boss! Don't pretend you're shocked at that; it happens all the time! Look at all the people that they are connected with and make note of the titles that may fall into an area of what your products or services may support. Your "sales training" should give you some idea of those areas. Add those people to your spreadsheet as well. If you're lucky you may find a few that even have an email or phone number in their profiles, and you can reach out to do an introduction. If not, you can send them a LinkedIn connection invite and see if they accept.

TIP Getting new business contacts like this on LinkedIn takes a little tact. I would suggest that first you follow those people you want to connect with. On LinkedIn, not literally! Following them will allow you to see the types of posts they make and what kind of articles they re-post. This gives you an idea of what's important to them both inside and outside of the company. When you see a pattern, again going back to you being a detective looking for clues, like and comment on those posts. Follow up shortly thereafter with a connection request that references the post you liked.

Obviously, you want to say something positive in your comment, everyone loves a subtle compliment after all. It doesn't always work but it probably has a better hit rate than just sending random invites. Remember to make notes in your spreadsheet with dates and attempts at connecting. Also, check with your management to see if your company has LinkedIn Navigator (or other tools) which is a great tool to find additional contacts and provides decent networking links.

What do you do if the contacts you are finding on LinkedIn don't have good contact information in their profiles? Or if you search on a name that someone gave you for a company and find multiple contacts (John Smith) for that name? What I like to do in those situations is to Google that person's name with the city that the office/company is in. That can help you narrow down the search especially if John Smith is actually Jonathan Smith. Searching this way can also lead to phone numbers and more importantly these days, email addresses. If you don't find names searching in the specific city the company is in, widen your search to include smaller cities nearby. For example, if a company is in Atlanta, search in the surrounding towns like Alpharetta etc. I know this may sound a little extra, but it is part of building contacts, and then sales. You will get into a flow doing these kinds of searches and will get better over time as you'll learn which search terms work best for your area. AI (which we will discuss later) will also help in this. As AI matures, you may be able to create prompts that search for a list of contacts based on specific criteria that the natural language search will help with. Also, remember AI learns with every new version so don't just do it once and move on. You may need to do it multiple times with different prompts over a period of time to get more information. There are also a multitude of AI engines now that you can try and utilize so don't just stop with ChatGPT. Try Grok, or Perplexity, or Claude, or any of the several others that are available at the time of this writing.

Earlier I mentioned the 80/20 rule. The 80/20 rule is well known in sales. 80% of your revenue comes from 20% of your customers. What are the reasons though that you can't drive more revenue from the other 80%? You'll hear the usual responses, the competition owns that account, they don't have any money yada-yada-yada. The reality is that most reps are looking for the path of least resistance to making their quotas. If an account is known not to purchase from your company, the salesperson will make a small almost ceremonial attempt at developing sales there. Then when a sale doesn't come quickly, they just mark it down as having "tried" and they move on. You need to make developing new contacts in all your accounts a major part of your "plan" which most salespeople don't do. The biggest reason that you're missing out on revenue from the other 80% is lack of contacts and relationships. Contacts and relationships that you don't have because your sales team doesn't know how to build them from scratch. As I have mentioned, companies try to hire people with a large network. However, you will rarely find multiple reps that that many contacts The skill of cold calling and developing accounts is something that must be taught.

I know many of you will have teams of business development reps and lead development reps that will do this type of work for you. If the company's revenue supports those roles great! But it doesn't necessarily get you the contacts and relationships you are looking for. Many people in different companies do not want to work through sales adjacent people.

No matter what the sales trainers tell you, cold calling is the number one skill you must know in order to make it in sales. You must be relentless and consistent as you fill out that spreadsheet, as you can never have too many contacts (keep thinking Network). One thing to note is that cold calling is different across different industries and the products or solutions that you will sell. Often people think of the "Boiler Room"[6] or "Glengarry Glenn Ross"[7] when it comes to cold calling. Where are the Glengarry leads!!! You may find yourself in situations where what you are selling is dependent upon a massive cold calling effort. Only you can decide if this is the type of sales that you want to be in. Some companies do the cold calling for you with inside sales or lead development teams and hand off to outside sales, but some don't. You need to understand the type of sales you are signing up for as this isn't for everyone. In Business-to-business sales (B2B) you usually won't have those boiler rooms environments, but you may occasionally have cold call days as a part of a marketing push. Generally, though once you're established with your base that process turns into simply sending out mass emails on occasion, at least in my experience. Scripts will normally be pre-written for you from the marketing department for cold calling days but for those times that you are on your own its best just to keep it simple.

For emails I usually use something like the image on the next page. It doesn't really matter how you address the intended target. You could use "Mr. Smith" etc. Just do something that is professional but simple to grab their attention, that's what really matters.

---

[6] Boiler Room is a movie about an investment firm from 2000

[7] Glengarry Glenn Ross is a movie about real estate sales from 1992

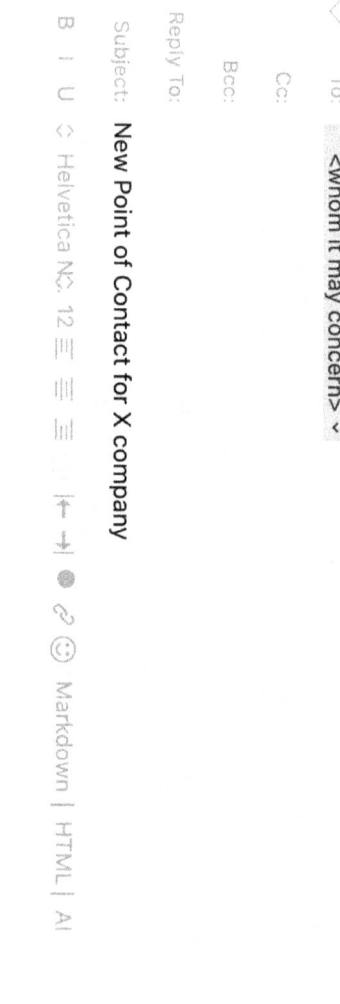

To: <whom it may concern>

Cc:

Bcc:

Reply To:

Subject: New Point of Contact for X company

Dear Sir/Ma'am:

Hope you are doing well! Just wanted to reach out and let you know that I am your new POC for X company. Would you have some time on your calendar for a quick introduction in the next few weeks?

Thank You or Kind Regards!

Name
Company
Phone#
Email Address

When sending introductory emails, you are trying to accomplish a couple things. The biggest, in my opinion, is showing that you respect the contact's time. Your email should be succinct and to the point. The potential customers don't want to read a novel, especially for just an introduction. Second, you should try to be informative. This person doesn't know you. If they had a sales representative previously they might not know that their former representative had moved on. Or they may not have had contact with your company before. Sometimes a customer doesn't know that your company can have an impact on their business, and this opens a door that may not have necessarily been available previously. You will want to note the dates that you sent the original email on your spreadsheet and put a reminder on your calendar to follow up in a couple weeks. Not a day, not a week, but a couple weeks as the people you're trying to connect with do have jobs and may not be in a hurry to respond.

TIP On following up on emails that have not been responded to after a couple of weeks try this. Forward your sent message to the contact and add "re:" in the subject field. So, in this example you'll send "re: New point of contact". It's a little subversive because it looks like a reply but sometimes you need that extra edge.

Once you've established some continuing communication with someone over email do not think that now you can now start sending novels to people. Many senior contacts will see lengthy emails like that and completely gloss over them, may not respond, and probably won't read any attachment you send. Keep your emails short and provide some bullet points to convey detail if needed. Adding some attachments is okay but again a library is not acceptable at this point. If you grab their attention with the bullets, they are more likely to read the attachments you send.

TIP Remember that you don't necessarily want to answer all their questions via email. Your goal should be to generate another meeting.

TIP Another reason not to add too many or too large of attachments is that you don't know what the company's email policy is for attachments. You may send documents that are too big and the email may bounce back. That causes delays and often missed communication opportunities that you must clean up later.

One last big thing you need to understand from your contacts once you've started building a relationship is how they like to communicate. Some still like the phone, some text, but most still want you to use email. You'll need to figure that out to maintain consistent communication!

TIP Face to face is still and always will be the most important thing you can do in sales communications!

Once upon a time, we used to call the main phone number at a company's corporate headquarters to try and get meetings. If you are dealing with some smaller businesses this is still a viable alternative to get a contact. Most of the larger companies will have too many levels of gate keepers for this to work anymore but if you are running out of options you can always try it.

TIP If you are able to make contact with someone's administrative assistant, treat these people like gold! Over time they will become an awesome resource for you.

CHAPTER 3

The Network

Another huge part of successful selling and one that companies will pay you extra for is your network. This can be more important than anything your resume or work history may show as it details that famous line of "It's not what you know but who you know". A network is a flexible asset in your tool belt as the people in your network move around, changing jobs and changing ideas. The network is full of humans so everything can change at any minute including whether they will remain a solid part of your network or not. You will see in LinkedIn where people have 500+ contacts. Contacts do not equal a network though. I can't tell you how many "contacts" I have that have absolutely nothing to do with what my "network" is. I made certain contacts to get a new job, to meet new people, and to gain access to their "networks". Sound a little brutal? Welcome to the game because other people are doing the same thing to you! Some people are pushing the boundaries of the "social" nature of business networking as a means of selling and advertising. Yes, there are "likes" in business networking too. Selling yourself is just as or more important than selling your products. Only you can determine if social selling is a path for you and if it will work in your current role. No harm in trying.

Developing your network is not something that happens overnight. It will take you a long time to build it so be patient. Unlike Instagram or other social networks, you don't just pop up and add thousands of followers overnight. It takes a career to grow and develop so again be patient and be active in the pursuit.

The next area to start your networking investigation is with your partner community. Companies normally have multiple types of partners that they work with. In the IT community companies work with distribution partners, consulting and technology partners as well as reseller partners. Part of your investigation is to identify the types of partners your company uses (if any). Check to see if you have some level of a partner manager that can help you identify those partners and maybe different tiers of partners. Cisco, for example, has all the types of partners listed above where AWS had some that were similar but focused more on the consulting companies.

What you want to do is work with the partner manager (again if you have one) to identify those partners that may support your accounts. Many of these partner companies may want to work with you on your accounts but not all would or should be engaged with your targets. Because of that you want to make sure you know their specific status with the client. The partners with active engagements are more than likely on good terms with the customer (though not always) and can provide you with some solid introductions. They may also bring you in on some meetings if you show value. Conversely, if you are working for a partner company in this situation simply flip the script. You may have to go to your bigger suppliers and ask them to engage you into the account which they may or may not want to do. If they don't it may be because they may have someone else in there doing the same or similar work. Those companies may not want to muddy the water with another partner.

While this is a solid method to get access you need to understand that the people your partners are working with may not necessarily be the people you need. They may be adjacent to what type of contacts you need. This is because your partner could be selling more than just your company's products/solutions. This will require you to continue your investigating but will be slightly easier because now you're in the door to a degree. You may find that the partner's primary contact can purchase something from this partner, but they may not have the ability or need to buy something from you. We often ran into a scenario where the partners had good contacts with the purchasing group at a company but didn't have relationships with the actual decision makers in the accounts. Make sure you understand the nuance of their relationships. A big thing to understand about working with partners is that you need to balance your desire to sell your wares with your partners' similar need to sell their own. Mutual respect needs to be developed with your partners in this respect. More importantly is an understanding that you won't try and push your partners to sell things that does not help them. This could negatively impact the relationships with the partner. A good partner relationship can last for years and be very lucrative for both sides.

A couple of questions you need to ask yourself when establishing relationships. One, is the person you are trying to develop a relationship with the actual decision maker or do they just like the attention? Two, do they have complete purchasing authority, or do they have to go to their superiors for approval? Often, you'll find contacts that have a certain level of purchasing authority but will need to go up the chain for larger deal approval. Be careful how much time you spend with those people that do not have this ability. One caveat in this scenario. Sometimes you will find an organization that relies on "influencers", not Instagram models but those people that are relied on by decision makers to help them make decisions. Those are people you absolutely need to develop relationships with. This grassroots method often leads to much deeper relationships and much more consistent sales over time.

Another way to develop your network is through events. Many companies will participate in industry events tailored to their customer base. Sometimes these are large conventions where you may get to experience booth duty. That means you get to staff the booth on the floor of the convention and answer questions from everyone that walks up all day. If you get lucky though, you may get to walk the floor of the convention to meet other people that have their own booth duty schedule. Other times there may be smaller events or seminars with very specific topics that your company may host or support. These are usually decided upon by the company's marketing department (or by salespeople begging management to let them go, it will happen). These events are essentially a place to utilize a specific amount of the marketing budget for the year to lure in sales opportunities. The marketing department or you as sales (or both) will be provided with invitations to send out via email or snail mail. Often marketing will buy lists of customers contact information to expand your company's base of customers for this type of event. The pros of this are that you will get a great number of leads, but you will have to convert those leads to meetings and ultimately sales. What does this mean for you? more research! The rates of conversions to sales from these events aren't spectacular but even a small percentage increase can be helpful, and those numbers will be used to determine the next or next year's participation in similar events.

Once you have developed a list of target contacts you will want to start your outreach just like we did with cold calling. Do some quick research on the contacts then develop an introductory email. The one we used in cold calling will work just fine. For this type of outreach, it's still important to keep it short and to the point. The reason now is you're not exactly sure if this person is even a decision maker you will need and you won't know until you get a response. Sometimes you may even need to meet with them to find that out which isn't bad because it will give you an opportunity to ask for the type of contact you are looking for. Often you may need to customize the emails for these contacts. For example, if a contact reached out to your company for information after visiting an event, you may want to add some additional information that coincides with their request, but again don't go heavy. As I've mentioned previously, many executives are looking for the hook and if they don't see it right away will just pass your email by if you send them too much.

Just like in cold calling, you will want to go through the follow up process by noting the dates that you sent the email and put a reminder on your calendar to follow up in a couple weeks. If you haven't heard back after two weeks though you should try the forwarding trick I described earlier as well. If you don't receive a response after that wait three or four weeks before the next attempt.

TIP Remember to put reminders for follow-up on your calendar.

If you don't get a response after that you may need to shelve that contact for a retry at a future date. Don't discount a long term follow up email. You never know when some new information may cause a potential contact to change their mind about meeting with you.

For the next couple days or weeks, you wait patiently or impatiently for replies but you will wait. The idea behind all this is that you will spend a large amount of time developing this pipeline of contacts. Over time you will turn contacts into relationship, build your network, and then perhaps sales. How does that glamorous sales job sound so far? It is a lot of work and if you have a large customer base it will be a continual thing for quite a while.

CHAPTER 4

The Real Work

As Bruce Buffer says, "It's time!" You have finally gotten those first contacts and meetings set up. It's time for you to prove you can close some business! Well sort of, you're not just going to walk in and get handed a purchase order unless you are amazingly lucky! If that's the case you should go buy a lottery ticket too.

In this next part, you will find that it's not that easy, but it is time for the most important part of being a salesperson. It's time to Shut up and Listen! Most sales training classes will instruct you be on offense when going into meetings with your customers. Their idea is for you to project strength! Obviously, your company and now you know what's best for your customer! You know you have the best products and solutions! So, by definition you should know what your customers need more than they do! And that is completely wrong!

Your customer is taking time out of their busy schedule to meet with you for a reason and that reason is not for you to tell them your new products or services will fix everything that ails them. They are taking that time to meet with you and to discuss how your products MIGHT, and I emphasize MIGHT fit into their current operations and potential needs. Your goal in your first meeting and probably in the next several meetings is to gain an understanding of your new customer's business directly from them. Not to tell them what you WANT to sell them. Herein lies another hard left turn in sales. This goes against most of the over-the-top training programs out there. The way I teach it, your first goal is to gain a small sliver of trust with your new contact and listening to them is how you get that started. You want to gain as much information about them, their roles, and business operations as possible. Through these discussions you will learn what the business needs and how your company can best work with theirs. You can't do that if you are pushing products right out of the gate. So put away the laptop, ditch the PowerPoint slides, and get out your pen or stylus and start by having a discussion and taking notes.

As I've mentioned, salespeople are always in intelligence gathering mode. This time, instead of getting the contact info you are getting information on the specific contact, the business needs, and as I've mentioned before, how they like to communicate. This is where you dive into a path of critical thinking. You will want to ask open-ended questions about what they do and what their responsibilities are.

TIP Situations will arise where you will realize that the people you are talking to can't or won't be able to buy what you are selling. While not ideal, it does happen. What you can do in this situation is try and identify areas in the company adjacent to that area and the people you are speaking with. People are usually more open to providing contacts in the other areas when you are sitting in front of them.

This ties back to your original information gathering on the company and building up your knowledge so you can have an intelligent conversation about their business. You will need to have a high level understanding of what they do already so you can ask intelligent and relevant questions. This is so the contact recognizes that you're not a used car salesman and are interested in what they, as a company, are trying to accomplish. By asking open-ended questions and letting the customer speak, you will often find greater opportunities. If you simply go into these initial discussions with the singular thought of selling a product you may miss out on larger opportunities. Conversely, you will also find a quicker path to understand if your products and services are NOT a fit with this company at all and save yourself some time. I've been in meetings where I've only asked maybe three or four questions, and my customer spoke for an hour! It'll take some trial and error on your part to figure out what works best for you. Only you will understand how to modify your delivery with your personality, but in the long run you will be much more successful if you start with this track. Regardless of the direction the discussion moves in though always take copious notes.

TIP Don't be let down if a first meeting is only 15 to 30 minutes. This is fine for an introductory meeting. Getting face time with a customer will lead to more meetings.

TIP This is where the W's come in. Why, where, when, what and who; these are the questions you will need to get answers for. Why is the customer doing this? When are they doing it, where will the solution go (not always on the list), what have they done so far and what will this impact. Who is involved both internally and externally including the decision makers. The last one is the non-W question, <u>how</u> does this get the customer to their business objective.

This may sound like it is counter intuitive, that you're wasting your time. The sales trainers tell you to charge hard and ask for the sale at every opportunity, challenge the customer! To some sales trainers and many managers, it's a numbers game. The more you ask, the more meetings, the more challenges, the greater the chance of success. Being overly aggressive increases the chances that you won't have an opportunity for another meeting. These trainers post a picture when they institute their type of training showing metrics and close ratios, but never what the long-term effect of this type of aggressiveness has on the customer/company relationship. They also don't consider the impact on future sales. This is often why there is also a high turnover in sales. Both salespeople and their customers get burnt out by this constant type of pressure. These trainers still go by the adage of diamonds are only made with high pressure! You'll find that with patience and perseverance you will win more and you will become a high performer. You will also last in your sales career much longer. The way I look at it, I'd rather not sell a tree this week but close a deal on the entire forest later. Patience leads to bigger paychecks!

Back to your meeting though. Part of this method is also to determine where the person you are meeting fits into the organization and does this person have purchasing ability. A friend of mine had this one question he always asked himself, "can this person buy a pencil?". That is something you definitely need to figure out. Maybe they can buy one, but can they buy the box? If they can buy the box, can they buy a case etc. Obviously, this isn't something that you ask directly. You must use your sleuthing skills and critical thinking to figure this out from multiple meetings. This includes talking to others in the company and to your partners to get to the right answer. Sometimes that answer is no, they can't buy a pencil, but they may be instrumental in helping the decision maker make that decision. These are influencers, and as I've mentioned before, can be more impactful than the person that signs off on a deal. They are often the ones in the trenches that report up the chain exactly what's making the clock tick and stay on time or tick and be completely off. This is something else you'll figure out after several meetings. I have had great relationships with influencers that have led to sales relationships that lasted for years because the influencers were more open to the ideas we provided. Because of this they would bubble the ideas up to management. While they can't buy the pencil you still need to nurture these relationships to be successful. Also, these influencers are often long-term employees within these companies. They tend to stay much longer than the upwardly mobile executives.

The larger goal of all this is to become a "trusted advisor" to not just the influencers and their leadership, but to the company. This goal takes a long time and is a hard-fought position to attain. One area within companies that can sidetrack this is the purchasing side of the house. You will run into scenarios where purchasing and sometimes other teams have the role of playing overseer and roadblock. Many companies will compensate these groups to negotiate lower prices or to prevent companies from having too much of a portion of a company's spend in any particular purchasing area. You'll hear terms like two party solutions where companies keep two vendors for a solution in order to have negotiating power over both. It's also a protective measure for the company in case of a major incident with a single vendor. On the other hand, the people in purchasing can end up being a better advocate for you than those you thought would be your key contacts. It's all about developing relationships at every level you can.

In thinking of this idea of the "trusted advisor" you want to be sure you really understand what the relationship with your contacts is. You may like the people you are dealing with and they might like you, but you aren't looking for "friends". You must maintain a level of dispassion with being in a sales role. You aren't being fake, but you do have to walk the fine line of doing your job and protecting your company's position along with providing the best possible solutions to your customer. You should look at this as a "feelings vs. facts" type of situation. If you're getting ready to close a competitive deal, you can't base that solely on a belief that your customer loves you. Feelings don't win over facts! The fact is that relationships may only buy a couple points of cost difference if you are lucky. Maybe your solution is "good enough" for the price but does it completely fit the need? In the end, the facts will determine the outcome.

I was competing for a large deal with my biggest customer. My competition had relationships on par with mine and with a specific member of leadership. I'd say they had an even better relationship with a certain decision maker. They had a solution on par with mine, but we were significantly more expensive. Again, sometimes you can overcome a little price difference, but this was massive. We had to circle the wagons and drive the customer to do an apples for apples comparison to make sure they were looking at this correctly. We lined up all our experts, prepared all our facts, and chatted with all our contacts to make sure we hadn't missed anything. When we presented our case to the senior leadership at this customer, we were able to show that the competition, while appearing much less expensive on the overall solution was significantly <u>more</u> expensive because they left out some important details. They were omitting the details of some adjacent pieces that should have been included in their pricing but wasn't. We didn't catch the competition lying per se, we just had all the specific facts on our side. The facts led to our winning the deal. Facts almost always win over feelings in sales.

Remember, you don't become the trusted advisor from being amusing, paying for lunches and happy hours, though it helps! You become that person by helping solve business problems.

TIP Part of selling and selling well is understanding the difference between perception and perspective. You may perceive that you know what your customer wants or needs. It may be instinctive to follow that direction but that's incorrect. You need to put aside your perception and instead try and understand the customers' perspective. How do they view their problem, how do they view your solution, how does it fit into their process, larger vision, and business outcome. Basically, you need to put yourself in their shoes and try and understand everything from their point of view. You can only do this is you know your facts!

Let's say yay great, you won a big deal! The success you're looking for is not that you just won a big deal, but in the process, did you establish a deeper relationship? When we won the deal I just mentioned we had already been at the level of the "trusted advisor", but after the deal this was firm. We showed that we just weren't pushing our products for our own benefit, but that we had the best solution for their needs and provided them will all the possible outcomes that were good and bad. We didn't hide anything. Competition, no matter the level, usually cannot win battles if they can't win on the facts. Even in light of extreme financial differences, reaching a customer by showing you are in sync with their long-term business outcomes will give you the edge. One thing though, don't let it go to your head. As you gained it, you can lose it. We had a saying in the Navy, one "oh-shit" eliminates all "atta-boys".

Thinking about business relationships, one thought should always be in the back of your mind. Some of these people you are working with will not be in their roles or even at the company you're calling on in the future. For whatever reason, they may leave and the implications of that can be large. First and foremost, what do you do when your primary champion leaves? Who and what are your backup plans? This is a big reason why you cannot rely on just one person to be "the champion" at a company. You will always need not only that primary champion but several secondaries. If your champion turns out to be a rock star in their field, other companies may try to steal them to be a leader for their company. You will want to make sure, like your knowledge of what you sell, that your relationships with your customers are both deep and wide. You don't want to wake up one morning, before a deal is about to be signed, only to find out that the person you expected to sign on the dotted line has left. Not only will that cause a large setback for you and your deal but also with your standing with this customer. Especially if no one else knows the conditions and status of your deal. Just another reason why heat maps are important!

Knowing your customer also means knowing their meeting preferences. This is similar to the communication discussion earlier. Do they like in-person meetings or does video work for them. Do they want meetings or calls on Mondays? Do they prefer not to talk at all on Fridays? You need to know this about your customer. The same regarding their purchasing process. How long does it take to get an order through their processes? Do they only order the end of the month or the quarter? Do they often have funds available for end of the year purchases? What do you need to do to be prepared to handle that? Have you noticed yet that everything keeps coming back to attention to detail!

TIP Take this to heart, never setup a meeting if the goal can be accomplished with a quick call or email.

I mentioned we'd revisit LinkedIn. Not only is it a great research tool, it is also a great communication and sales tool BUT you must be careful with it as well. You may see some great information from your company or a partner on a post and want to share with your customer. Hopefully you've already connected with your customer on the platform, if not do it quickly. Since you're already connected to them in person skip the normal LinkedIn process I mentioned previously and just send a connection request. Using this type of communication also requires understanding and discussion with your customer. (See previous discussion on communication) Is this the type of communication they are interested in? Do they find this helpful or annoying. Don't assume just because they are on the platform and connected with you that it's ok to spam them. Go back and re-read what I told you regarding lengthy emails.

A little story about knowing your customer's processes. I worked with a large telecommunications company that we did multiple millions a year in revenue with. Every year in late October or early November they would have end of year budget/funds free up. However, in order to use those funds for capital equipment purchases they had to have the equipment delivered to them physically before midnight December 31st. One year I received a call from an architectural planner informing me that they needed 85 pieces of gear that they had standardized on and had purchased previously.   Knowing something like this would probably pop up we had already spoken with the business unit within our company that was responsible for that piece of equipment and we basically reserved a large number of units early in the fourth quarter. We weren't prepared for that huge amount though, so we had to beg, borrow, and steal from some other accounts in order to satisfy that order. The quotes and other paperwork took a couple of weeks, which didn't leave us much lead time to get the orders packed and shipped by the end of the year. To give some scope, only two of these items would fit on a pallet! As we were coming down to the wire, I had one of my co-workers literally sitting on this customer's warehouse dock on New Year's Eve waiting for the truck to show up. I was getting calls every hour or so from my director and the CIO for this division of this company right up to the point where my co-worker called to let me know that the truck had arrived with a good 45 minutes to spare! The multi-million-dollar order that significantly impacted two different companies after two months came down to 45 minutes. Just a little stressful! Think about how this would have impacted our company if we didn't know and understand this customer's processes? Had we not known their trends of big end-of-year orders we would have been up a creek without a paddle!

This opens the door to that executive sponsor discussion. The executive sponsor is usually an executive from your company that may have a background in your client's business. Looking at it from the client perspective, they are looking for a senior executive from your company that has a title associated with their name that they would consider a peer. Think that a CIO would like to have a relationship with your CIO or maybe just a VP level to VP level. These types of relationship can be very beneficial, especially for customer satisfaction. The client, knowing they can reach out directly to this executive sponsor, provides them with a feeling of empowerment. It takes away, somewhat, from the direct sales team but can have long-term benefits if the executives are properly aligned. That is the tricky part and sales should have input on the executive assigned. In my example with the telecommunications company, my director was the executive sponsor contact for this customer. He had a multi-year relationship with the CIO so it was an obvious fit.

Internal to the customer, a salesperson wants something similar to the executive sponsor, but we call that person on the client side the sales champion. (we also use the term executive sponsor but don't want to confuse the topic) This is the person that is helping to push your products or solution within the customer because your selling convinced him already. Generally, you'll want someone more senior, when possible, to help you. This person will already be convinced that they want to work with you. They may be part of your Network from a previous role, or you cultivated the relationship at this client and were able to bring them aboard with your ideas.

What about the competition? The competition is always there, they will always try to win just like you will. Be better, know the facts and know the competition better than they know themselves!

CHAPTER 5

Presenting the Story

Once you've gathered all your intel, investigated and defined the needs of your customer, it's time to do some of the less hardcore aspects of sales. At least it's less in my opinion. Time to learn how to do presentations.

Depending on the company you work for, the marketing department or the product teams will have people that put together presentations as a part of their roles. You may also have people that will do the presentations to your customers for you for specific products or solutions. However, these presentations aren't always the best things to share. They are often very detailed with busy slides and usually too many slides. While certain situations require detailed presentations, training on a product for example, doing an introductory presentation or high level product presentation does not need that much detail. These presentation decks from the marketing department are usually overkill and will probably bore your audience to tears, which is not the start you're looking for.

To get the biggest bang for your buck on this type of initial presentation you want to greatly simplify the message. Taking some of the data points you gathered from your investigation phase, which I will keep mentioning, you will want to integrate some of these points to show how your solutions impact your customer's business and the needs that you identified. This shows the customers that you're not just regurgitating canned information and that you've listened to their needs. Remember that if you're delivering this to business leaders they care about bottom line and outcomes. How does this impact the profit or loss of the company, how does it make their business better, and how does it fix their problems. It's not just an answer that you're better than the next guy. You need to make sure you really understand what the most important thing for these leaders is in respect to your offering. If you're delivering to a specific line of business, whether its HR or a machining division, tailor your delivery to what's important to them. Again, it's about what they need and how you can help them. Even if your company is the 800-pound gorilla in the your industry you need to be humble. It's fine to reference other companies that use your solution but again you must show how it fits <u>this</u> company's business. You'll have certain people telling you to push hard, show confidence but you'll find being more conversational, more collaborative will gain you greater adoption from your customers. Just shut up and listen!

Crafting your presentation takes thought, not just deleting the extra slides. You want to make sure your company's message is clear. This doesn't take an overly detailed slide to complete. Keep it simple, that's why company slogans are succinct. When you get to the meat of the presentation you'll want to follow this same thought. Keep it simple. You must look at presentations as the telling of a story. You'll need to do some background study on your audience so you don't bore them with useless information, but you also need to make sure you're not talking past them. Using images in lieu of overly detailed text and talking about your company/solution in relation to the image works quite well. What do I mean by this? If your company's products will increase the velocity of another business's ability to deliver their products then put in an image with the relation of speed. For instance a cheetah or image of lightning, then speak to that image describing how your company does that. Replacing heavily detailed text with an image keeps their attention, where text, especially overly detailed text in a small font to get all the data on one slide will bore people. You'll want to save slides like that for deep dives with people that are more concerned with the specifications of a given solution than the high-level decision makers. Presenting this way reinforces to the customer that you know your own solutions and how they can help the customer's outcomes.

I keep bringing up decision makers, remember we identified the decision makers as the person that can buy a pencil. Make a note of the people in the room that are curious about value during a meeting as they will usually be the people that you want to target. Often the senior most person in the room won't ask too many questions, if they do awesome but if they don't, don't take it as a negative. In large companies, the leadership rely on their key people for recommendations, as we've discussed. They may not be fully engaged in a presentation. Don't let that sway your focus though as there will be others in the room that are. This is how delegation works.

TIP Make sure you can tie real numbers to your solution in presentations and not pie in the sky theories. For instance, if your product or solution can increase productivity by 25% to 35% don't go in there with 50% to 100%. I'm a firm believer in under-promise and over-deliver. Go the other way at your own peril.

Remember that the ultimate goal of a presentation is to convey information, not necessarily to close a sale. Make sure you complete the task that you expressed initially to get the presentation. Like a good story, you need a beginning, middle and end. Don't abruptly end the presentation without having some type of call to action. Whether it is something you will do for follow up like providing additional data or product pricing. It may also be something the customer needs to provide for you to complete your task for them or at the very least asking for a follow up meeting.

This may seem like an odd place to put this comment but while I wasn't quite sure where to put this in the book, the presentation area seems to be fitting. It is a topic that while many would see as common sense, but some need a good smack on the back of the head to realize it. Salespeople are often well dressed and tailored because, as I've said before, you're selling yourself as well as a product. Sometimes they get a little overconfident in their looks and how they present themselves. You want to dress to impress but you need to know your audience. Don't show up to a meeting in a $2000 suit when the audience is in jeans and vice versa. I've known many salespeople over the years that have flaunted their success and ended up paying for it over time. Just because you can afford to drive a BMW doesn't mean you should show up to or worse, pick up a customer for a lunch that can't afford something like that.

It has a twofold effect. One is that it can have a negative impact on your relationship with your customer. Maybe not outwardly but when a competitive situation arises, they may think you make too much money compared to them, and this is the power they hold. Preventing you from getting a deal and maybe future deals. Secondly, it may limit your future relationship with that person and that company. The converse of this is that maybe the people you are dealing with are higher up the food chain than you are and have a higher standard of living. Don't try and play keeping up with the

Jones' just because you "think" you should, it won't help you with those more senior people. You'd like to think that personal feelings aren't a part of a business decision, but they definitely can be. What's the net? Just be careful you don't overdo it once you get to a level of success. Remember that at the end of the business day your customers may go home to vastly different worlds.

A few words on how personalities across geographies differ and impact business relationships. Often you will bring in experts from around the country to help you present. Being from the Midwest I've been told everything from I don't have an accent to I sound like a country boy, but the biggest things is that Midwesterners are generally considered polite and amicable. Not sure about using those two to describe myself but in general many people from this neck of the woods are looked at in that way and can generally fit in anywhere. However, there are a couple areas in the country where people, how do I say this nicely, come off a little different. To be straight, salespeople from the east coast don't necessarily work well in say Iowa. Similarly, salespeople from Chicago don't necessarily work well in Texas. I'm picking on these two specific areas for a reason and have a couple stories to tell about them. Personality types in those areas work very well, in those areas. However, if you go to the heartland, or the South and you may not have as much luck. This is an over generalization but something to be considered with regard to territories. If you go to work for a New York based company, you may want to ask how the previous salesperson from New York did if he was calling on Houston.

We have a couple multi-national companies here locally that I've done business with over the years. My direct manager and I were close to closing a large deal when our VP from Chicago decided that he needed to fly in and close the deal for us. The senior leader at this multi-national took our meeting and for about an hour listened to this VP "instruct" him on why he needed to sign with us. You could feel the tension in the room the whole time. At the end of our time our VP asked for the order and our contact looked him straight in the face and said, "If I decided to award your company the business I will work that out with the local team". As we walked out of his office our VP stopped at the bathroom and our contact told us to never bring him back again. His condescending attitude really put off our contact and he did not appreciate being "told" what he should do by someone that's never been in his building before.

We had another situation where an East Coast consultant was brought in to discuss the financial impacts of a solution we were working on with the CFO of a large company. During his presentation he took a similar stance to what the VP I described in the last example. He preceded to inform the CFO that the large companies he works with in New York follow a specific direction when working with the type of financial solutions we were discussing and basically told the CFO that her team was not working in an informed manner. The CFO stopped the meeting, told the consultant that while his points were interesting, that "we do things differently in the part of the country", thanked him and had him leave the meeting.

The last thing on this topic is etiquette, I know, groan. You'd be surprised how things have degraded with regard to basic etiquette, especially in meetings. For me this is a real deal killer. If you can't respect your customers, how will they respect you? Be present in meetings and leave your cell phone in your pocket. If you are taking notes on your computer, make sure you are making eye contact with the people that are speaking so they know that you are invested in their topic. This is basic, but this seems to be the norm in the digital age and just the state of business these days, people are forgetting these basic forms of etiquette in meetings.

TIP When taking all this in, a bit of advice. Just like top athletes, there is a fine line between confidence and arrogance. The fact driven confident salesperson will succeed where the arrogant and emotional one will fail.

CHAPTER 6

Negotiating & Closing

I must address something before I get into the details with this piece. When I read other books, some by very famous authors of very popular business books, I laugh at the ways they talk about closing a deal. Some examples of these are: The Assumptive Close, the Pressure Close, the Soft Close, the Presidential Close! Every time I hear or see these types of "closes" it reminds me of a quote from Oceans 11[8] the George Clooney version. They had a scene when they spoke of a litany of hustles. The quote is "Off the top of my head I'd say you're looking at a Boesky, a Jim Brown, a Miss Daisy, two Jethro's and a Leon Spinks, not to mention the biggest Ella Fitzgerald every!" It just cracks me up!

---

[8] Oceans 11 a heist movie involving a Casino from 2001

Deals are won and lost for a variety of reasons. Anywhere from cost, product fit, and the history of the business relationship. Experienced companies will do all their due diligence on a major product purchase internally and at times will bring in external advisors to negotiate on their behalf and/or provide consulting to the decision makers. As I've stated multiple times the facts need to be on your side to provide you with the best chance of closing a deal. Even with all your ducks in a row a savvy customer may pick the other guy because they "negotiated" something that you couldn't or wouldn't provide.

Make sure when you are in a head-to-head battle with another company you fall back on a three step "facts" argument. First, establish with your customer that you understand their current business situation (Fact 1). Second, that you also understand what their future state needs to be (Fact 2). Third, how your solution best gets them to this business outcome better than the others (Fact 3). If you can do this, you will put yourself in a position to win. Many companies including Amazon do what's called working backwards. Which is a similar thought process. This is where you define the business outcome and using your solution work backwards to the customer's current state to see how you can show what gaps exist and fill in the steps in between.

Negotiations can be complicated because of any number of things. Pricing, delivery times, warranty all have an impact. Often winning or losing a deal may simply be that the customer can't afford your product/solution as you priced it. You and your company will often have to make difficult decisions when it comes to price in these situations. The customer may really want your solution but just can't afford it. They may not be open to different financing methods or just aren't willing to tie up a large amount of funds. Companies have any number of different reasons, and you can be prepared for most but there may be situations where you just can't meet their demands no matter what you try and do. That leads to an always difficult scenario where you and your company may just need to walk away from a deal.

A question that your company needs to determine: What is more important, to win the deal at a potential loss after a big investment of time and resources. Or to lose the deal to maintain your level of margin and value for your company? If you bow to the customer demands, they may expect you to do that in future negotiations or product renewals down the line. Only you and your company can decide what's more important. In these situations, you also run the risk of the deal information leaking out to your competitors and could impact future clients. If you think companies don't leak information or your "buddy" in purchasing is doing you a solid by sharing information to you and no one else, you are in a big world of denial. Don't misunderstand me, many companies will take bad deals at significant discounts depending on the time of the year. As I said, it comes down to what's more important at the time.

In situations like this where you may be looking to take the deal at a loss you have a couple options. You can propose to build growth into the deal for future or ongoing purchases to get you back to "whole". Some companies will do this just as a point of not wanting to lose any business. This also shows your management that the customer is really invested in working with you and not just going for the cheapest solution. Playing the long game like this is risky but has its rewards if you're willing to roll the dice. I don't advise it as an ongoing business strategy because once you cave in on pricing once the assumption from the customer is you will do it again. The other option is to simply say thank and walk away. Companies will do this when they believe they have a strong hand. The expectation is that the customer will come back to the table. Another famous sales line during negotiations after the deal is offered is "the first one to talk loses". This does have roots in reality though. If the customer speaks first usually the sales guy wins, if the sales guy speaks the door opens to more negotiations.

Another risky strategy is what we refer to as "calling the baby ugly". Sometimes you will have a product or solution that is a perfect fit for a customer, will absolutely help them and they just don't get it. They think they have everything under control and nothing you are proposing will make a difference. This is where you gently tell them that they are wrong, which many people will find offensive. Usually this will happen either with founders at the top or at the middle management layer. Middle management types can develop personalities of omnipotence when they have been king (or queen) over the domain you are working to sell to. They will not want to admit in any way that they have made any mistakes. As I said, this is very risky and you may want to try and use the good cop bad cop method on this. (Just like the movies) Bring in someone else to be the bad cop in this situation so you can continue to maintain the relationship later.

Sometimes you lose. Yes, just like your dad told you, sometimes you are just going to lose a deal. It may be because of the price, it maybe because of relationship, or it may be because the client just can't do the deal. On one occasion we were working with a healthcare company on a long-term deal. We went back and forth negotiating price, length of term, products involved and consulting services for months. Everyone that could possibly be involved was involved on both sides. The customer at one point brought in one of the third-party negotiators I mentioned to try and get a better deal than we were offering. They ended up throwing in the towel because we were at the absolute best anyone could give them. At this point, you'd think that everything was in our favor, and we were just waiting for a signature, right? Well, that's what we thought too but the customer and the decision makers decided they didn't want to assign all the risk to themselves, so they pulled their board of directors into the conversation. What happened was a lose-lose for both of us. Their board decided that the money would be better spent in another area during this fiscal year. Everyone on our side lost, didn't matter what the title was, what the forecast was, no one was to blame. We just lost because of a situation completely out of our control. We took the hit, and we moved on, nothing else we could do. It did affect a couple people on the team who pretty much packed it in after the loss expecting to get a great check out of the deal. The thing about sales is not that you necessarily have to negotiate with your customer for every deal, but you also must consider the negotiations you have within your own company with your own team. You will need to make alias within your own company to help you get deals done.

TIP Often you will be told to "ask for the deal". Sometimes this is an option but most times it's not in large B2B sales. You will want to come to an agreement with your customer on an outcome and that will include a deal. This doesn't mean it's a "win-win" situation. The customer may get what they want "mostly" and you may get what you want "mostly" but you both probably caved in on something.

CHAPTER 7

The Best Part - Getting Paid

As I've said before, compensation drives behavior. One of the biggest reasons people get into sales is simply for the money. When you talk to recruiters, they will always have a pitch that starts out with something like "our top rep made" and it's some ridiculous number that maybe one person in the whole company actually made when the reality is something very different. I've chatted about the base salary and the mundane tasks that are associated with that, but the real dollars are tied up in the variable side of the pay, the commission, bonus, and maybe stock plans. Each company is different, but the fundamentals are the same. You will get assigned a quota based on their compensation plan/territory and from that you will get commissions and bonuses. The main thing you need to get out of this is that you need to understand the number they give you to make the money they promised you! A very important lesson with compensation plans is that you need to know EXACTLY how you get paid.

"Rules are what separate us from the animals" Winston from John Wick.[9]

Why do I bring up Mr. Wick? Throughout that series of movies there was always a constant reminder about rules. It is the same in sales but in sales knowing the rules is about getting paid! You must know the rules about how you're being paid and how your quota is broken down! To make money it always helps to make your assigned quota but it's not the only way to make money.

Companies have a habit of burying the details of the current year's compensation plan assuming that salespeople won't pay attention to the details or take the time to understand all of them. These companies pay accountants large sums of money to make complicated algorithms to make sure you don't understand. Normally you will have a top line number, the total amount of your sales for the year that you must make. But things are never that simple. You may have "buckets" that you need to fill with the different types of things you sell. You get paid more for things in bucket "A" than you do for things in bucket "B". Let's look at it like this. You sell apples and oranges. Your company wants you to sell 150 pieces of fruit, 100 apples and 50 oranges but oranges are more expensive and harder to come by this year. For every four dollars of oranges, you sell you get two dollars in commission but for every four dollars in apples you sell you get one dollar because they are more available this year. You sell 150 apples and no oranges therefore you met your quota of 150 pieces of fruit, right? Not necessarily because you didn't read all the details of the compensation plan. While the plan initially said "sell 150 pieces of

---

[9] John Wick is a movie starring Keanu Reeves 2014

fruit" you think you're good but buried in a paragraph deep in your plan it says that you max out on commissions for apples at a quantity of 125 when no oranges are sold. Even though you hit the top line number you can't max out the compensation because you didn't sell any oranges. This is the type of thing that drives salespeople crazy, at least the ones that don't pay enough attention to the details. You will find this type of detail at any number of companies. So, you need to make sure you understand fully what you have signed up for and plan accordingly.

A little story, I worked with someone who was a very average salesperson. Never really blew out his number but always came in close, and close is good enough to keep your job, every year. He knew all the ins and outs of every part of the annual compensation plans down to the penny. Every program, every possible bonus and he did just enough to get every one of them. That was his thing, he didn't care to be the number one guy he just wanted to get to his number, protect his job and maximize his cash. He knew the level of work he had to do to get there and didn't care what anyone thought of him. My point with that example is you have a choice, you can be handed a quota, not pay attention to the details, and see what happens or you can be like my former peer and maximize all the revenue available to you in the plan. The third option is to maximize the revenue available in the plan, plan out your year to manipulate the compensation plan in your favor, and be a high performer. Management sets up the rules of the game and let's face it, it is just a game. Once you know the rules inside and out, it's time to look at your customer base and determine who can help you reach your goals and how.

One customer may need to buy a lot of apples, the other a lot of oranges, another may need pears. Plan to maximize the sales across your account base regardless of what any one customer needs. See the 80/20 rule!

Make sure when you are discussing or negotiating your offer for a sales role that you understand the package that they are offering too. Is this a 50/50, 40/60, 70/30 package? Meaning that the salary is the first number (percentage) and the commission is the second. Thus on a 50/50 plan you will make, for example: 50,000.00 base salary and 50,000.00 commission at 100% of your quota. Details on how they get to that and any upside usually rolls into the compensation plan which you probably won't see until you get hired. Big things to understand here, the bigger the salary normally the lower the total upside if you get beyond the 50/50 type split. It's a choice you must make, do you feel better about having a big salary or would you rather have an exceptional ability to get to the upside (or more) of the commission plan because you won't get both in my experience.

TIP This may seem like a feast or famine type of thing but once you have a firm grasp of the job and know your territory, you'll be able to plan better on the money you make. It may take a year or two to figure it out, but you will. One thing I see many reps do though is to not save their money for the off years. This then turns things into a feast and famine situation when it doesn't have to be! You will have bad years, assuming one in every three will not be great so manage your business and your money so that the off year doesn't destroy your bank account!

Many companies think they have figured out the way this new world of top salespeople works but good salespeople understand this and are a step ahead. For example, you may be provided with a reachable goal, meaning you'll hit between 85 and 101% of your number two out of every three years unless something unusual happens. For the top reps, they can blow that "reachable" number out of the water one or two of those three years by doing what I described in the compensation section, knowing exactly how to get paid. That means that one of the three years they probably won't make the quota. No matter what they say, it's planned that way. Consider that one year as a make-up for the company. If you do have a blowout year you can fully expect that you will have a quota the next year that you just can't make. Many salespeople will see this coming, change roles, and even companies every few years because they know they won't make any money in that off year. They'd rather roll the dice doing something else that has a potential of making money than staying in a role that has a high probability of not making any. Pick your battles!

CHAPTER 8

Sales Management & Training

First and foremost, just because a person is a good or great salesperson does not mean they will be a good sales manager. Salespeople are often a different breed for a variety of reasons and depending on those reasons, the movement to management can turn out to be extremely limiting. Taking a "one size fits all" approach to managing any team rarely works, Yes they all have certain tasks that have to be done month in and month out but apart from that you are dealing with a variety of personalities that need to be nurtured independently of each other. A manager that tries to make the entire team "in their own image" is most likely a recipe for failure.

These days it takes letting go of certain theories about how a great salesperson is developed. Often sales managers look for people that are just like them and that is a bad path to go down. They are basically trying to hire a similar personality type repeatedly, never breaking the circle. That may and probably is not the best way to have an elite salesforce. I keep using the term additive. You need to find people that are additive to existing skill sets, not just mirroring the skill sets of other people. When you use the method of "just like Mike"[10] you often find that while they are close to Mike, they are still Tom and Tom's personality by default makes his process different.

A good manager evaluates each person independently and will direct them based on their own strengths and weaknesses. A manager must empower salespeople, not micromanage them, to get the most out of a team. A key idea with this thought is that high performers will raise the bar of the team by X%. Conversely, lower performers can bring the team down by a similar percentage. [11]

This requires a manager to look carefully at their team and to make adjustments to that team over time. You will always have rockstars and slackers on your team. (See next chapter) You just need to minimize the downside when you can. When you are a sales manager, you must continually work to help your team improve their skills to improve their careers. Just setting up a calendar appointment for once a month check in to see how they're doing adds little value. Without providing them with feedback or providing them with some type of direction on how they are performing, the team and everyone on the team will not benefit at all.

---

[10] Refers to Michael Jordan

[11] https://insight.kellogg.northwestern.edu/article/sitting-near-a-high-performer-can-make-you-better-at-your-job

As you make the choices for hiring managers as well as salespeople keep something in mind. Unless you have direct knowledge of each person you need to be skeptical of their abilities. Especially with internal transfers. I've been in many situations where it was in someone's own interest to move an individual up and/or laterally to remove them from an organization. This will happen for a few reasons, the least of which is a person may have been hired by a certain manager and that manager became embarrassed by the bad decision. Instead of letting the person go they move them so they can keep their own reputation intact. Good for them, bad for the company. We call this screw up and move up. Other similar situations exist where someone would like to move up quickly in an organization and they are moved into different roles to learn more about the company. They have a "protector" that sees themselves as a mentor. They will identify someone, maybe someone did it for them, and put all their chips in on this person. Regardless of their skill set they may be in a place where they aren't qualified and will disrupt that area. In sales this can be quite a problem as it impacts not only personnel but customers and the bottom line. They may only be in that role a short time before they move on to disrupt some other area but are in the role long enough to cause long setbacks due to the inexperience. Google the term "post turtle".

This seems to be a good spot to start discussing training. Throughout my career I've been relegated to some of the most inane training you can imagine. Whether it is the "sales methodology of the week" training or just inadequate training for a specific role, it continues to baffle me that companies don't recognize the wasted time and money that goes on with training salespeople. A question that needs to be asked is "Does this training directly reflect what my salesperson will be doing on a day to day basis and will it increase this person's ability to close sales rapidly?" The answer in most cases is a resounding no.

Let's look as this in two parts, one with seasoned/experienced sales professionals and the other with those new in role. The training for those new in the role needs to be much more in depth. Not only does the training need to include training on the primary products/services that the company sells but also the tools that are needed to do that role. Think CRM (Customer Relationship Management) as well as an on-the-job training period of time where the new hire shadows senior sales people to see the processes they use to sell, document, and process orders. This would include internal tools, contacts such as in finance or technical support or whatever is needed to properly process orders. This list could be exhaustive depending on the company, but do you want to train the salesperson to be out the door and selling quickly while making serious mistakes? I'd rather take some extra time to make sure they are locked in and ready to go. Just make sure you don't overdue the training to the point where it's too overloaded and the salesperson misses or forgets half of it.

The following is a failure of most companies. Regardless of the experience of the person you MUST spend the appropriate amount of time to train the salespeople to your company's methods and expectations. I've seen and been a part of organizations that run you through firehose training for a week then give you a laptop and throw you to the void to sell. The idea being you were hired as a professional so you should be good to go with just the basics of the company otherwise why are they paying you the big bucks?

A difference between the professionals and the new in role should also be noted and acknowledged. While the initial training remains the same the messaging to the experienced professionals should be different. During the shadowing period the professional hires must understand that the point of having them go on shadow calls is merely a way for them to get acclimated more quickly to the processes and culture of their new company.

This goes hand in hand with the hiring of the right sales manager. You must vet a person well to make sure of their skill set and that they are a fit for this type of role. You can check their references, which is usually a sketchy bet as they won't give you someone that isn't going to say good things about them. During the interview, delve into actual situations where they have had to develop an account from the ground up as a salesperson vs taking over an already established account. Also discuss situations where they've managed people before. You'll need an understanding of what their processes are and how or if they can fit into your company's sales methodology. Make sure the metrics you assign are solid and clearly understood so they can be held accountable. The carrot and a stick methodology, while not the ideal thing these days, still works. Having specific training conversations with prospective new hires is important. You will need these so you can understand what type of investment you may need to make in a particular candidate. This should be a part of your hiring process. Do they know how to cold call? Can they develop relationships outside of their area of expertise? Do they have the needed attention to detail skill set to do the job you need them to do. If they don't, are they trainable? If they aren't trainable and unless they are bringing an amazing book of business with them, you may need to pass.

In defining your company's approach to training, I don't advise the firehose method. Most people won't retain all the information you throw at them in their first weeks. This leaves them prone to mistakes early in their role. Too much training and overly high expectation setting can cause the reps to rethink the role and leave if it makes them uncomfortable or not confident in delivering the message. The advice we give is not to push a boot camp type of training. Rather build knowledge on an ongoing basis over a period of time. I'm sure many of you are saying we already do ongoing training on a monthly/quarterly basis. That's not the same thing and I'll explain to you why the way you are probably doing that isn't having the impact you think it is having. To get your new people integrated, you need to provide a better learning environment. Once you get through the first day of HR related activities such as getting them a laptop, a desk if you do that and make sure everything works. Don't just hand them things and tell them to go to a website and follow a series of steps. While some companies think this automated /self-service training is great, "we have a portal!" It can be intimidating to even the most senior people. For some senior people it can put undue stress on them because they will be the people LESS likely to ask for help.

You will need someone to help them onboard, in person or on video conference, so that they understand their role. You may have to designate one of your team as a sales training advisor. This is not an official trainer, just someone that knows the job, knows the correct way to use the tools and any internal processes that the new rep will need to understand initially. Basically, a sales buddy but you want to make sure that this person isn't just checking boxes with his additional duties or you will have a new rep with the bad habits of his "buddy".

Once the new rep meets these first steps, plan their first 90 days with them and set expectations and milestones for them to reach during this time. This isn't a "trial" period but a "break-in" period where they have extra help on just about everything from products, processes, systems and everything else down to expenses. Nothing upsets a salesperson more than not knowing how to get expenses paid and having to fumble through a bad tool to get mileage and expenses paid for! During the first weeks you will want to have the new hire's days scheduled with different exercises, not all classroom or online training! Nothing is less productive and less effective than being power pointed to death in a conference room!

Break the training days up. For example, training on Tuesday morning with sessions lasting 35 to 45 minutes with breaks between each session. Provide long QA periods after every couple of classes, with people that can answer questions on things like products and services or scenarios where these things fit together in solutions. One thing here that I want to make sure you understand, this is NOT a place for ROLE playing! Role playing is the biggest waste of time and money ever! I'll rant about that more shortly.

As the initial weeks move forward, switch the days up so that it's not the same schedule every day. If they start with products and services on the first morning, on the second have them sit in on the sales meetings, or other meetings that they may need to be a part of. It also helps for them to be in sales adjacent group's meetings that may support sales in some way, so they understand a day in the life of everyone they'll be working with.

One of the strongest training methods that I suggest is on-the-job training. On-the-job training used to be prevalent in every type of job but for some reason sales trainers stopped using it. Which is odd as it can accelerate the new hire's ability to be productive and revenue generating. Part of this piece is developing a shadowing schedule. You should have the new hires scheduled to go to meetings with multiple existing/experienced sales reps for them to see what and how each person handles their meetings. This provides them with a greater scope on the job, the company and generates more questions. It also prevents them (hopefully) from making one person's process their own. Multiple versions of how to do the job gives them better information to learn how to develop their own process. We believe this type of on-the-job training is invaluable and should be integrated for every new hire. This should be a tracked exercise over the 90-day (or longer) period. A debrief meeting should also be included after every customer meeting that the new hire "shadows" to answer all questions for the new hire. Lots of "why/how" questions will come out of these meetings. Why sell this with that, how do you get that ordered that way, when does it get shipped, how do we deliver etc. Having this debrief provides the new sales rep with a detailed learning experience. The output of which can be taken back to the manager or trainer. Debriefs should happen on a weekly or biweekly basis to go through the questions in an open setting. A specific day just to go through those details. With senior salespeople you will have a similar training regimen, but the ramp will be much quicker. Do not force senior people into training meant for those first in role. They will zone out of most of the training, and you'll have different issues because of it.

Ongoing training is something that all companies will do, however companies often try to put a square peg in a round hole. Not all training is needed for all employees unless the company thinks this is "the way", yes that was a Mandalorian[12] reference. If that is the case, don't send out some virtual, self-paced training. People will find ways around it or through it and it won't have the effect you wanted it to have. I speak from experience avoiding that! Instead provide a live training session for those cases but please NO ROLE PLAYING! That rant is coming. Putting out a list of training sessions with no carrot at the end of the stick doesn't do much. Remember salespeople are coin operated, put something out there that they feel will be worth their time. Whether it's a quarterly bonus for keeping up with these trainings or some type of "reward" will go much further than an extra icon to add to their personal web page. Time is money, don't waste the time of the people that you've hired to bring in the money!

Ok, now my diatribe on role playing. Role playing is what training groups within companies or "training consultants" provide when they have nothing relevant to share. Let's role play a fictitious sales situation with the CFO of a fictitious company and go over objection handling! Ugh! I call tell you from my over 30 years of experience that NOTHING you do in a "role playing" scenario will ever happen or prepare you for what may happen. Don't waste time or money on organizations that pitch this as a "tool" for salespeople. Objection handling is something you learn over time and by seeing other people do it in real situations which role playing cannot do! You have to be in the room and paying

---

[12] The Mandalorian is a TV Series on Disney+

attention to how people react physically and emotionally in order to understand. Taking canned responses from role playing into real situations is a recipe for disaster. I can hear sales trainers rolling their eyes right now. The role-playing scenarios shouldn't be taken to a customer word for word. It's a guide! Blah, blah, blah, it doesn't work that way in the real world!

For Example, I had a meeting with an International Contracts manager at a large conglomerate with my sales manager. We walked into a huge wood paneled conference room where we sat and waited for 30 minutes. The customer came in, didn't shake our hands or do any type of "hi how are you" he just sat back in his chair. My manager started talking to him about what we were there to discuss. At one point, the customer leaned forward, pulled out a pack of cigarettes (yes cigarettes) lit one, and then told my manager to shut up! He then proceeded to tell us, well mostly my manager, how he had no intention of ever working with us because of a prior situation that caused him pain. Show me a role-playing training where THAT comes up! The last point in training, I promise, is that you can never stop training. Even if your company isn't providing anything new, you need to seek things out on your own.

TIP One thing to remember about sales is that you may choose sales as a career but the place you are working is more than likely just a job. You must remember that your sales career will take you to other jobs so never stop investing in yourself and increasing your value!

Another lovely part of sales that you will experience every year are reviews. They are a normal part of sales management, and annual reviews are a necessity. It's the time when the company reflects, I mean scrutinizes, your performance for the year. Did you make your quota, did you come close, or did you miss badly? Good reviews (and reviewers) also look at the challenges you faced through the year. Did anything outside of your control affect your sales, like acquisitions or other issues with your customer base. Also, how well did you work with others? Were you supportive of your peers? Were you collaborative? As I mentioned earlier, GE would do annual reviews and then take the bottom 10% and let them go regardless of what they brought in. You'll need to decide the best way to handle these reviews. Whether your company is like GE or not, do you have a way to determine if good employees can become great employees through different training? Reviews aren't just a lower-level employee function, it's something that takes place throughout an organization. 360-degree reviews let employees provide a level of review to their management. It's a helpful tool but it often isn't used correctly. These are often instantiated as anonymous surveys. The problem with this though is that the surveys can be skewed by one unhappy employee or by poorly designed survey structure.

Another part of sales management to understand is the sales cycle. Make sure sales management understands and communicates not only what your company's sales, manufacturing processes and logistics capabilities are but what each of your client's purchasing processes and schedules are as well. Not all companies purchase things the same way or on the same schedule so you must be able to adjust forecast models once you understand this. Making monthly or quarterly forecasts when a customer is on a 12-to-18-month schedule can make things overly complex. Best to understand in the beginning vs later and adjust your forecast and potentially your leaderships forecast. I have seen managers push sales reps to enter an end of quarter or end of year deal because they want their direct management to see that there is potential of making or exceeding a number (quota). This sets a dangerous precedent for several reasons. The biggest of which is making a salesperson think that no matter whether you think you can close that deal in that time frame or not, you should have it in the quarter/year. If you miss or must push the deal to another month, then there is a domino effect that runs uphill which makes everyone in that sales chain look bad. Better to have a deal out in the next quarter and pull it in than the opposite. Some will argue but from a business perspective this is a sounder way of doing things.

Recognition of this is a good start but building an organization that has these skills is something else. Teaching old dogs new tricks is tough because they don't want to learn, they like things the way they are. How many of your sales team, if you ask them, would tell you they made their number with the way they've been doing things for years so why are you asking them to change now. That's fine if you just want account managers, people that just babysit accounts that are going to buy your products no matter what. No matter the price, no matter the warranty or the quality. It's the old adage of "no one has ever been fired for buying IBM". That's fine if you're happy with mediocrity. That's why lazy companies structure their sales the way they do. You have 10 sales reps, the total quota assigned to those reps is $1 million. The manager above those reps has a quote of $750k, so he needs an average of 75% blended from the 10. Now you have 10 sales managers with a quota of $7.5 million and the director above those 10 needs only 75% of the $7.5 million. Keep this working until you get to the boss and that original $100k per rep quota is down to $56k by the time it reaches the top. Good thing most reps don't ask those kinds of questions. You're back to a group of people that may have two or three solid salespeople and the rest just get by, but that's okay because the numbers always work out or get close to working out.

What if you could change that 56% back up to 75%? Wouldn't that be worth some amount of training and some amount of change? You just must deal with the eventual and expected complaints of certain members of the team that will be complaining regardless. This isn't some mad scientist experiment; it is simply instituting a function of sales that has always been there but has recently been left behind.

Lastly, when you hire what you believe to be top tier salespeople how do you determine that they actually are the top tier? It's not like you're calling their former bosses to see if they made quota. Your HR people are checking resumes and LinkedIn and making educated guesses. I'm sure you have some level of interviews that you hope are culling the not so experienced but are they asking the truly important questions about the fundamentals of the sales process? Or do you just have your canned process with psychological profiling included that are supposed to tell you if they "fit" your ecosystem? How many windows are on a block where the average height of a building is 10 stories and there are 80 windows per floor? Who cares! The question that needs to be asked is can this person develop an account? This is more important to me than whether someone "fits" the culture.

CHAPTER 9

The Legacy Sales Rep

In the history of sales, you will run into 3 types of sales reps. "A" players, the top of the food chain, are very hard workers but super high maintenance. They are great to have on the team but mess with their compensation at all and they will exit very quickly. The "B" players are the people who do "just enough" to make their number but will never have the drive to do more than just that. These are also the one that will keep asking to have more. Lastly, the "C" players. These people are happy with getting by on their base salaries. They have great golf handicaps, usually are on the expense naughty list and always whine about something or someone. They occasionally make their numbers but only do the basics of their jobs. The unfortunate thing is that you have to go through a period of wasted time until you discover what types of salespeople you have and then another period to get rid of them through administrative processes which can take months.

Don't misunderstand though, while the A players are mostly focused on making the most money they can, all salespeople will be looking for the door if you start messing around with their money. Good salespeople will know the best way to maximize their compensation. Whether it's straight sales, sales contests, SPIFs, bonuses, they always find a path. If you start reducing the ability of a salesperson to make the living they were originally promised they won't be around long. There are so many variables to different companies' finance models and compensation models that we won't get into detail on compensation plans just know that salespeople are coin operated and no coin, no operation.

Continuing the theme of sales rep types, recognition is also on the list for driving behavior. In addition to money, some want their name's in lights. They want to have their name read off the list for chairman's club or whatever you may call the top performers list in a given year. They want that prize too, the trip to Hawaii or the bonus check which depends on your company's generosity with the sales team. Some salespeople don't care about this recognition; they just want the cash. Many want both, but you'll have to decide which are the most valuable to your organization and how to manage their expectations.

A big benefit of hiring "professional" salespeople is that they can work well in certain levels of autonomy which many companies need because of remote work. I'm not just talking about working from home vs. the office though we need to address that too. Many people in sales, but not all, enjoy sales because of the freedom it provides. Get your sales calls done, your paperwork updated, close a deal and voila you have free time. Some of us used our roles to spend more quality time with our families. I "worked" from numerous sporting events of my son's. I didn't shirk my work, but I made sure that I got my work done in a way that allowed me to schedule my time to be at my son's games. The whole "work life balance" for me revolved around that for the last 18 years. I made sure that I scheduled my travel strategically, especially on trips where flights were involved so I didn't miss much. Prior to that I didn't care how much travel had or to where I had to travel. Companies embrace this type of salesperson because they need to. They don't have the resources to have offices in every city.

Some salespeople, and you'll know who they are, push the limits of how much they must actually work and get away with it. They do the minimum and are happy with that but are also first to complain about having to do anything additional or having anything change that impacts their created lifestyle. Most of these people have single digit handicaps and/or really nice cars, they like to brag about everything. There are also those that push the boundaries of the expense reports, trying to stay in the nicest hotels, eating at the best restaurants, basically living a life way outside their means and charging it back to the company. They are usually on the expense naughty list but always seem to sneak by due to working the system. It's always a challenge determining what kind of salespeople you have but the evidence always presents itself in one way or another.

When you are offered an opportunity to work remotely or work from home think about a couple things. One, how good are you at managing your time alone? Will you be able to deal with the distractions at home? Two, can you separate your work-at-home life from your life? Some people don't do well working remote. They need interaction with others in person. Some do better because they utilize the lack of distractions that remote work can provide.

TIP If you work remotely the best thing you can do for yourself is set a schedule and stick to it. For me the schedule is simple, times are flexible but it's important to get into a routine. Always enter tasks, events and activities into the calendar though. Don't assume you will just "do" what you planned; it helps to have the visual.

Sample Daily Calendar:

October 9, 2024
Wednesday

- **6:30 AM** Workout, Breakfast, Shower
- **8:30 AM** Email/Paperwork
- **10 AM** Meetings/Calls
- **12 PM** Lunch
- **1:15 PM** Meetings/Calls

Let's close with this thought. You get what you pay for. If you are looking for solid sales reps that will consistently make their quota and raise the proverbial bar you have to pay them. Thinking you can game this system never ends well. Pay your people at industry rates or above rates and that will be the first step in them working harder for you.

CHAPTER 10

Sales Tools & Process

For those new to sales, I'm going to give some broad-brush strokes on sales tools in a salesperson's everyday life. Broadly CRM is the main sales tool, however companies have a habit of bringing in way too many communication and data management tools which just overly complicate every process. I may go off the rails a bit in this section as I believe it can become a crutch for companies that don't want to make proper investment.

Email will always be needed; it is the primary means of communication both internal and external. It is a way to share data and keep records of multiple conversations. Currently there is a love affair with serial communication tools like Slack. Nothing against it, it's a fine tool. But it's a difficult tool to use as a document management solution. Salespeople have better things to do with their time then to learn how to write a script in order to find a copy of a PowerPoint. After that you'll probably see SharePoint and then Teams or Webex, because why have one conferencing tool when you can have three. What you need to consider is how many of these tools tie into your primary tool and in what way that will help you? In CRM you're asked to track meetings, but can you import meetings from Outlook? Slack is owned by Salesforce but does two-way communication between the two tools actually work seamlessly? Have you been trained on how to use it? Are all the proper conduits in place for the two tools to be additive to each other? How do you fix it if it's not? Always tough questions that are usually above the pay grade of sales managers and sales representatives.

Company's toolsets are usually tied to the senior level management at the time. When new management comes in to a company they often bring new tools and processes that they believe have worked well for them previously. This usually causes a degree of historical data loss and disruption to operations when changes are made. Not to mention how it affects employees which really isn't considered. Especially when not enough time or attention is given to resetting expectations and proper training.

When choosing tools for a sales organization, Salesforce.com or whatever CRM is being used, companies tend to make the data entry forms overly complicated. They overpopulate them with all types of datapoints. While the idea is to have a single source of truth for all of sales and marketing the tools often become overburdened.   This leads to the sales teams not wanting to populate them with usable data or using them at all. Trying to track the value of every marketing program through these tools will never provide true actionable or reportable values on the products (or programs) associated with them because sales will skip or just "check boxes" to move orders or quotes along in the process. Many companies overlook the integration and ease of use pieces of these tools when acquiring them or they don't want to pay to have those extra features and benefits enabled. If you want this type of tool to be that single source of truth, your CMDB for my technical folks, you must put the time and effort into the tool and the training of the people that will be using it.

Some simple solutions would be to install better SKUs, better product descriptions and make sure those are kept up to date by your operations people. Eliminate products or tag products in the tool that are scheduled for sunset with forecasted dates for sunsetting that is shared with the sales team. Dropping a product at the last minute with no warning will get you sales team satisfaction issues in a hurry! Doing things this way, reports can be simplified, and additional value will be driven from marketing based on outputs from the tools Limiting the amount of inputs required from the seller along with hyper accurate SKUs/products should provide better accuracy for forecasting.

Contracts, organization charts, and heat maps should all be part of these tools and not separate so all teams can provide inputs and updates which can then be tied into account plans which maintain that idea of a single source of truth. Doing everything in a tool and then outputting it to a document or spread sheet should only be necessary for certain types of presentations. This is also helpful when there is turnover as everything is in the tool and not spread out over multiple documents and file shares. Keep it simple but make sure it's mandatory.

Questions come up from salespeople on how much effort they need to put into these tools. Back to compensation drives behavior. As a manager, don't try and stand on "well your base pay covers your data entry in SFDC", that just won't work. The base is table stakes in competitive industries. Make it worth the salespersons time and don't over complicate it. Providing some type of bonus for multiple factors in the tools will get you more and better data. The top salesperson with the best percentage to close ratios gets an extra bonus! Keep the Starbuck's cards though, cash is king!

Determining what is actually needed in your CRM tool is tricky. You must balance the needs with the available data. What is the level of granularity on sales that your company needs? Only your company can determine this based on your historical sales. Do you have products and services that are sold to each of your customers daily, in other words extremely short sales cycles? Are you that transactional? Do you have long sales cycles? Quarterly or longer? And how do you tie that back to your internal systems for manufacturing or ordering. What are your lead times and how do sales affect that? Do you account for an "average" monthly sales cycles, shorter? Longer? Do you plan on a percentage of over buying or under buying based on your sales? If not, how do you do your internal forecasting? Maybe a percentage of growth month over month? These types of questions and cross-company collaboration is what is needed in order to develop a proper set of sales tools. If your sales tools are nothing more than a funnel and do not tie to internal systems in some way you might as well be using Excel.

On forecasting, how often do you need to see a forecast and how often do they need to be updated? Many companies use the rule that you should have two to three times the opportunities in a pipeline in order to make a given quota. It's a nice thought but most companies don't scrutinize these pipelines to the degree that every opportunity is going to generate revenue vs. just being in the pipeline to keep management happy. If I had a nickel for every time I heard a manager say things like "just put something in Q4 so the pipe looks better" I'd be a rich man. Don't be surprised! This is common place in big companies because many people care about the wrong things. Back to being coin operated.

Part of the problem is having too many or not enough sales stages in the tool. Also, not having nearly enough triggers to determine when something needs to be moved from one stage to another and in some cases backwards which almost no companies do! Say you have an opportunity working its way through the stages and the company runs into an issue with revenue. They still want your product, but it's now delayed. How do you track that? Well, you work around it because you can't move backwards which throws off algorithms that go off of "time to close" a deal and thus the forecast. And what are the downstream ramifications of that internally?

It's probably factual to say that your sales teams do not know what each stage means and what's attached to each, especially regarding timing. This goes back to the discussion on training. Companies have people that determine the "average time to close" of a normal deal and that gets built into the system. But do you teach your salespeople that information and the reasons behind it? The answer is no because you don't think that your salespeople need to know that information. There is often no review of opportunities to this level of granularity. It's usually only to the degree of "is the opportunity still relevant" or do you need to move it out or close it. Salespeople HATE closing opportunities because it means they must find another to replace it. They'd rather move it out a couple quarters and deal with it later. Often, you'll find that opportunities are re-named and re-used multiple times. How does that affect the algorithm? These are easy to find as the details usually don't match the name and the creation dates are usually REALLY old. So why do companies do this? Why do they allow it to happen and continue? I ask myself that regularly as it has never made sense and I think it comes back to the structure of the sales organization. Each level of manager only cares about, using an old acronym, WIN! What's important now. I don't remember who coined that, might have been the old Notre Dame Coach Lou Holtz, but I'm not sure. Anyway, each manager knows what details "their" management wants to see and on what time frame. They ask their teams for that information and no more. Why is that you ask? If you don't need more there's no point in filling up your inbox with extra crap.

Again, what does that lead to? An endless loop of crappy opportunities, re-treaded opportunities, and excuses. At some point in time, one would think that the operations side of the house would want this fixed as it throws off their internal forecasts. Or do they just assume that the sales team are normally wrong and use a simple process that works regardless of the sales team's input. Which will lead to other issues down the line like late orders. The sales team then must explain to the customer that is complaining about delayed deliveries impacting their processes. It's an endless loop that for some reason companies just don't want to deal with.

Wouldn't it make sense to streamline and scrutinize the process? Go through the pain once and get everyone on board, make the process a non-negotiable part of the day-to-day job of sales. Sounds too easy, doesn't it? But how much time and money is wasted because you don't have these processes in place? Would your close rates increase? Would your cost of sales decrease? It would make sense that your operational costs would also be better controlled just getting off the endless loop.

How do you do that then? You need to spend the time looking at your sales processes and determine how much simplification can be done. Do you need 8 sales stages or 4? Is your time to close 4 weeks or 8 weeks? Once you mine your own data, you can make the decisions. You know the problem and you know a version of the answer. You must determine the steps between these two and implement them. Don't do it in a vacuum though and don't create a "swat team". It must be all or nothing with every group involved. You may need to survey all the groups that touch the final product to make sure you get everything covered.

CHAPTER 11

The Cloud

This is an add-on to the Sales Tools discussion. Most companies have established themselves in the Cloud now, so I'd be remiss in not adding some comments to address that and some advice to working within the Cloud. First let's talk about the systems that run your company. How many of you are over investing in every type of software product because you want the best of breed for each area of your company. At one point or another decision makers decided, in their own silo, that this was the best-case scenario for the business. However, the costs associated with this for the overall company were not taken into consideration for any of the single purchases. These siloed decisions also didn't take into consideration the sharing of data or as common platform for the data and the ability to create reports. This results in additional costs for integration. Most companies don't review during the acquisition process how a major system will interact with another. This is usually an afterthought once someone asks for the data of one system to be integrated with another. At this point some type of solution is attempted, usually a duct tape version of a software conduit that only does part of what is needed. How can you develop the outcomes that you need when systems aren't compatible. This again falls into having a better communication strategy with all groups involved, one that looks towards the needs of the whole company and not just the siloes.

Regarding Cloud and trying to run pieces of your business in the cloud I'd like to offer some advice. As a Datacenter and Cloud Specialist with Cisco my role was to provide guidance to our customers on a "multi-cloud" strategy and as a Senior Sale Rep for AWS, well I think you get the idea. So, what's the advice? We'll keep it to the common sense idea and the keep it simple idea. What that means is that you must identify a few things first. What systems are mission critical to your business. Of those systems which are you willing to put into the cloud, and which are you not? What are the reasons behind that decision? If it's security, you need to accept that your team's ability to keep data secure pales in comparison with what the HyperScalers can do. (See AWS's Shared Responsibility model) If it's something else like general fear, keep it onsite. Financially you will pay more in the initial stages of moving to cloud, but you deal with the same thing with any large change. Cost models increase with initial acquisition and decline over time. That's always the pitch but it's up to the company to follow the guidance to keep that to be true.

TIP What most don't take into consideration for that line is growth. The cost goes down "if" nothing changes. If the company grows, data grows, costs go up.

The best advice in working with the cloud is do whatever you can with a SaaS model. This way your provider takes care of everything, and you just worry about your data. (Simplified answer) If you try and build your applications in the cloud or as "cloud ready" you are limiting your company to a number of things, not the least of which is locking yourself in with a single vendor. The big three cloud service providers offer easy and inexpensive ways of getting into the cloud, but they also have expansive services that you can sign up for. Your thought of "we're just putting containers in the cloud so our workloads can be portable" is only reasonable if you don't sign up for some of the proprietary tools that the providers offer. Once you start down that path, enjoy the ride with that provider if and until you're ready to take the hit to move. For some companies, they will just accept that they are there forever. It's the same with virtual machines though they are being pushed aside for containers.

To become "cloud first" you must embrace the multi-cloud scenario. Microsoft still owns the desktop, especially email, so you'll have an O365 contract, with that you'll have your exchange hosted as well and almost by default you will be using Teams. While it's debatable about how well Teams works, it should be good enough because of the integration. I have seen a company, again with major siloes, end up with contracts for Teams, Webex and Zoom because they didn't talk to each other internally. Webex was a legacy contract, Teams was acquired by the end user team during a software renewal, and Zoom was acquired by the telecommunications team who bought it with equipment they purchased for conference rooms. Now just think about how much money was wasted due to lack of communication. But I digress yet again. Continuing this path of cloud, you'd want to add salesforce.com (or another provider) for your CRM and utilize built-in plugins between that tool and Outlook to synchronize meetings and the data therein. I've been to several companies that use both but neither has thought far enough to do this integration and these were TECHNOLOGY companies! One did use Slack with Salesforce, thinking that the integration would be great because Salesforce owns slack, but guess what you just added another tool! Are you getting my point? Do your homework with cloud. Don't just listen to a "cloud consultant" or your "cloud guy". Ask for multiple levels of input, especially from your internal team on how things are working today and how they would like to see things work going forward. Operating in a vacuum will only lead to bigger problems and more unneeded expenses.

CHAPTER 12

AI: Savior or Skynet?

Artificial Intelligence (AI) has become a transformative force in many industries, and sales is no exception. The integration of AI into the sales process offers numerous benefits, from enhanced productivity to more personalized customer interactions. This chapter explores the various advantages of using AI in sales, supported by four practical examples of its application, while not a comprehensive list it does show the potential. Finally, we will discuss how AI can influence the 80/20 rule in sales and predict the percentage of time AI will save within the sales process.

Enhanced Customer Insights

One of the most significant benefits of using AI in the sales process is the ability to gain deeper customer insights. AI algorithms can analyze vast amounts of data from various sources, such as social media, customer interactions, and purchase histories, to identify patterns and trends. These insights enable sales teams to understand their customers better and tailor their strategies accordingly.

For example, Salesforce's AI tool, Einstein, analyzes customer data to predict future behavior and recommend the best actions for sales representatives. By understanding customer preferences and pain points, sales teams can create personalized experiences that increase customer satisfaction and loyalty.

Improved Lead Scoring and Qualification

Lead scoring and qualification are critical components of the sales process. AI can significantly enhance these tasks by automating the evaluation of leads based on predefined criteria and historical data. This ensures that sales representatives focus their efforts on the most promising prospects, improving efficiency and conversion rates.

An excellent example of this is HubSpot's AI-powered lead scoring system. The platform uses machine learning algorithms to analyze data from multiple sources and assign scores to leads based on their likelihood to convert. This allows sales teams to prioritize high-quality leads and allocate resources more effectively.

Automation of Repetitive Tasks

Sales representatives often spend a significant amount of time on repetitive tasks such as data entry, scheduling meetings, and sending follow-up emails. AI can automate these mundane activities, freeing up time for salespeople to focus on more strategic and revenue-generating tasks.

Conversica, an AI-powered sales assistant, exemplifies this benefit. The AI assistant can handle routine tasks such as contacting leads, following up on inquiries, and scheduling meetings. By automating these processes, sales teams can operate more efficiently and close deals faster.

Enhanced Personalization and Customer Engagement

Personalization is a key factor in successful sales strategies. AI enables sales teams to deliver highly personalized experiences by analyzing customer data and providing tailored recommendations. This level of personalization enhances customer engagement and increases the likelihood of conversion.

For instance, Amazon uses AI to personalize product recommendations based on customers' browsing and purchase histories. This not only improves the shopping experience but also drives higher sales. Similarly, AI-driven chatbots can provide personalized responses to customer inquiries, ensuring a seamless and engaging interaction.

Examples of AI Application in Sales

1. Predictive Analytics for Sales Forecasting

Predictive analytics, powered by AI, allows sales teams to forecast future sales with greater accuracy. By analyzing historical data and identifying trends, AI can predict sales outcomes and help organizations make informed decisions. This leads to better resource allocation, inventory management, and strategic planning.

2. AI-Powered Customer Relationship Management (CRM)

AI integration in CRM systems enhances their functionality by providing real-time insights and recommendations. AI can analyze customer interactions and suggest the best actions for sales representatives to take, improving the effectiveness of CRM strategies.

3. Chatbots for Customer Support and Lead Generation

AI-driven chatbots can handle a wide range of customer interactions, from answering common questions to qualifying leads. These chatbots are available 24/7, ensuring that customer inquiries are addressed promptly, leading to higher customer satisfaction and more opportunities for sales.

4. Sentiment Analysis for Customer Feedback

AI can analyze customer feedback from various sources, such as social media, reviews, and surveys, to gauge customer sentiment. This information is valuable for sales teams to understand customer perceptions and address any issues proactively. Positive sentiment can be leveraged to build stronger relationships, while negative sentiment can be mitigated through targeted interventions.

Potential Productivity Increases from AI Integration

The integration of AI into the sales process has the potential to significantly boost productivity. By automating repetitive tasks, enhancing customer insights, improving lead scoring, and providing personalized experiences, AI enables sales teams to operate more efficiently and effectively.

Impact on the 80/20 Rule in Sales

The 80/20 rule, also known as the Pareto Principle, states that roughly 80% of sales come from 20% of customers. AI can significantly impact this rule by optimizing the sales process and enabling sales teams to focus more effectively on high-value customers and prospects.

Identification of High-Value Customers

AI can analyze customer data to identify the top 20% of customers who contribute to 80% of the sales. This allows sales teams to allocate more resources and attention to these high-value customers, ensuring that their needs are met and their loyalty is maintained. By focusing on these key customers, sales teams can maximize revenue and strengthen customer relationships.

Enhanced Customer Segmentation

AI-driven analytics can segment customers based on various criteria, such as purchasing behavior, demographics, and engagement levels. This segmentation enables sales teams to create targeted strategies for different customer segments, ensuring that each group receives the most relevant and effective sales approach. By tailoring their efforts, sales teams can increase conversion rates and customer satisfaction across all segments.

Personalized Marketing Campaigns

AI can help design and execute personalized marketing campaigns that resonate with high-value customers. By analyzing customer preferences and behavior, AI can suggest the most effective marketing messages, channels, and timing. This personalization increases the likelihood of engagement and conversion, leading to higher sales from the top 20% of customers.

Predictive Maintenance and Upselling

AI can predict when high-value customers might need additional products or services, enabling sales teams to proactively offer relevant solutions. This predictive maintenance not only enhances customer satisfaction but also opens up opportunities for upselling and cross-selling. By anticipating customer needs, sales teams can drive additional revenue from existing customers.

Predicted Time Savings from AI in the Sales Process

Predicting the exact percentage of time AI will save within the sales process can be complex due to the varying nature of sales tasks and the specific AI tools employed. However, based on industry studies and expert insights, we can provide a reasonable estimation of time savings in different areas of the sales process.

1. Automation of Repetitive Tasks

AI can automate repetitive tasks such as data entry, scheduling meetings, and sending follow-up emails. These tasks typically consume a significant portion of a sales representative's time. According to a McKinsey report, automation can save up to 20-30% of the time spent on these activities.

Estimated Time Savings: 25%

2. Lead Scoring and Qualification

AI-enhanced lead scoring and qualification streamline the process of identifying high-potential leads. Traditional methods often require extensive manual analysis, whereas AI can quickly and accurately evaluate leads based on predefined criteria and historical data. This can save significant time and improve conversion rates.

Estimated Time Savings: 20%

3. Customer Insights and Analytics

AI-driven customer insights and analytics provide valuable information for sales strategies without the need for manual data analysis. AI can rapidly process large volumes of data to identify trends and patterns, enabling sales teams to make informed decisions more quickly.

Estimated Time Savings: 15%

4. Personalization and Customer Engagement

Personalizing interactions and engagement strategies with customers can be time-consuming when done manually. AI can automate the personalization process by analyzing customer data and tailoring communications and recommendations accordingly. This enhances customer engagement while saving time.

Estimated Time Savings: 20%

5. Predictive Analytics and Forecasting

Predictive analytics for sales forecasting can greatly reduce the time spent on planning and strategizing. AI can analyze historical data and predict future sales trends, providing sales teams with actionable insights without the need for extensive manual analysis.

Estimated Time Savings: 10%

Overall Time Savings Estimate

To estimate the overall time savings from AI integration in the sales process, we can combine the individual savings from each area:

1. Automation of Repetitive Tasks: 25%
2. Lead Scoring and Qualification: 20%
3. Customer Insights and Analytics: 15%
4. Personalization and Customer Engagement: 20%
5. Predictive Analytics and Forecasting: 10%

Let's assume that each of these areas contributes equally to the total sales process time. The weighted average of these percentages gives us an overall estimate of time savings.

Did you notice something a little different about this chapter? When you were reading it did it take a different tone in comparison to the rest of the book? Well, it should, I used ChatGPT (4) to write the beginning of this particular chapter. What better way to describe how AI can impact sales than asking AI to explain itself!

Now after thinking about this a bit, I've realized that I've been working in the technology industry for over 30 years! I may need to sit down for a minute or grab a nap. Ok, so my point is that I've seen, used, and sold most of the hot technologies that have been developed over a long period of time. Some have been amazing things that have changed the way we live and work. Some were just the latest "shiny new thing" that was cool for a minute and then faded away. It wasn't really that awesome or something better came along quicker not allowing the "shiny new thing" to get a strangle hold on an industry. As I'm typing this, I have CNBC on in the background. Many of the large tech stocks are reporting earnings and a huge amount of some companies' numbers are focused on AI. Most are reporting big swings and big misses because some got out over their skis on how much AI was going to impact everything this early in the AI cycle. This is my opinion but much of it has to do with the analyst community guessing on how AI would affect the markets and over driving the value of AI. "Bright Shiny Key" syndrome usually works its way through the system until everything is shaken out and the reality of what new technology can provide.

All that being said, from my view of AI or any new "disruptive" technology, I wouldn't normally get wrapped around the axle about it for the reasons I mentioned previously. However, when the amount of investment that has been poured into something the way it has with AI you really need to pay attention to it! Remember, we are VERY early in this cycle of AI. While AI/ML has been around for many years what we are experiencing now is leaps above what we've had previously both in software and hardware.

Strictly from a productivity standpoint AI is a game changer with regard to repetitive task replacement. I utilized a couple of very basic prompts in order to generate the first part of this chapter to show just what it can be used for according to its own opinion. Think about what you will be able to accomplish with some additional training! As you look over the examples of what ChatGPT thinks you can use AI for let's remember that for many a GPT[13] is the first real experience for the world to what AI is or can be.

AI/ML has been around for a long time now and has been in use by companies both large and small. At the time of the writing of this book, Jamie Dimon, CEO of JP Morgan, gave an interview on CNBC and the topic of AI came up. He said that they "currently" had over 2000 people working on AI and had over 400 use cases deployed! Mostly around the area of risk and fraud (makes sense), but I'm sure they've made use cases in sales as well. Sounds like a lot but he also commented that they had been working with AI/ML for about 10 years! This just shows that companies are already benefiting from AI but remember the famous adage, garbage in garbage out! AI can only provide answers and forecasts based on the data they are trained with. If you have bad data, you will have bad outcomes. This is where that massive investment piece for AI is coming from. Not just buying up all the Nvidia GPUs for servers but also scrubbing databases and building new ones to make sure that they are using the best data for better outcomes.

In my opinion, AI will never fully replace a salesperson in a true B2B setting, at least not in my career arc, but it will be an increasingly important tool for sales. I already know of companies

---

[13] a generative pre-trained transformer: a type of machine learning algorithm that uses deep learning and a large database of training text in order to generate new text in response to a user's prompt according to Dictionary.com

using AI for things like RFI/RFP construction and responses which is one of the biggest time sucks for any salesperson! You must accept that these tools aren't an option if you want to be a top performer! To reiterate, AI is a tool, but you must keep your skillset in using this tool up to date to be successful.

CHAPTER 14

The End Or the Beginning

As we are getting close to my self-imposed limit on pages for this book I must try and squeeze in a few more thoughts. Though it's not quite a summary I do think it redoubles what this entire text is trying to say about sales. Maybe I'm showing too much of my GenX with this chapter but again I think it shines a light on a few things that are important not just to those thinking about getting into sales but those that are here and looking to disrupt things to help make their companies better. In trying to change the status quo in sales we really need to understand how and why we got to this point.

Sales organizations have been pretty much stagnant since I entered the business world in the 90s. Siloed business units have been working towards their own goals. Ultimately, they all add to the engine of the company, but this structure is limiting. If all the units worked together synergistically, and communicated between each other they would drive much higher revenues. In effect, it is a broken model that does not change because the people that run them are all reading from the same book and paying same Ivy League consultants. It's time to break that model.

They say that in any organization eventually you will have to make it to a person at the top who is ultimately responsible for making the final decision. In the corporate world that is the CEO or president. You would think that this person would want people, processes and controls in place that requires each group within a company, each silo, to have to work towards a common goal. Wouldn't it make sense to structure compensation for reaching this common goal to drive better behavior? Doesn't it make sense to create that sense of community? Now don't get me wrong, I'm <u>firmly</u> in favor of merit-based compensation but the better a company works together the better the overall outcome for all employees. If you are giving bonuses to individual groups for doing just their part but not for collaboration your company is missing an opportunity. Companies are almost at war within their own walls and within these groups. I've seen it! Operations thinks they are better than purchasing, purchasing better than sales, sales better than marketing. Shouldn't there be more synergy? Or is this just an accepted gap in management theory? A gap that senior management doesn't realize exists or still believes that the internal competition drives performance.

I think the world of business has lost a step. Too many companies have become complacent. They've decided that in addition to making widgets they needed to be political, to be more inclusive and diverse. Whether it was being pushed down from the boards or pushed up through activist executives, it has backfired. The term go woke, go broke is now a thing because of this. ABInBev and Disney have both felt the brunt of doing things outside of their swim lanes. Things seem to be turning the corner a bit but it's time to go back to the things that made U.S. companies great! Back to the days of Neutron Jack with one caveat. During the days of Jack Welch at GE they created multiple silos within an organization. As I stated earlier, this is no longer a relevant strategy! Making these different groups compete just does not work in today's world. A company must have synergies across all levels of the business in order to be successful! We must return to being a merit based society, where being the best at what you do with the highest customer satisfaction is the way! (yes, another Mandalorian reference!) Surprisingly these two go together, who knew!? Like Jack Welch used to say, companies need to get back to the idea of being number one or number two in the industry and if not, get the hell out![14] Maybe that's a bit harsh but with that mentality you will win more. Is that ruthless? You're damn right it is but that is what it takes, at times, to be successful.

To utilize this methodology, you must first forget much of what you think you know. Wipe from your mind the overburdensome processes and procedures that you have grown to expect from sales teams of the past. They say repeating the same thing over and over again and expecting different results is the definition of insanity. Yet time after time, company after company, the same things are constantly repeated. That means most companies are insane or at the least they are below average.

Where do salespeople fit in with this idea? Companies often ask, "What do successful sales people have in common?" As we discussed earlier, the theory is that all sales people have certain characteristics that make them successful but what does that really tell you? Forget personality traits, forget trying to make robots based on a set of criteria you THINK is the ideal.

Companies are destined to fail when you try and pigeonhole people with different personalities and skills into the same cookie mold. How do I know this? We see companies bring in new sales methodologies every time they have a slowdown in business or a

---

[14] Three months after taking over as CEO, Welch set a vision for each business unit that they had to be #1 or #2 in their markets; if not, they had to fix, sell, or close the unit. This later became his one of the most famous strategies

major management change. All this does slow sales down. There may be a sudden pop of business with certain things but those increases could also just be normal part of the business cycle. Save the expense, maintain and nurture the tools you have and the people you have.

From Selling to VITO, Microsoft Spin Selling, Neural Linguistics or Challenger, we've pretty much seen it all when it comes to training. All these methods are heavily process based, check all the boxes and you will win! That has proven time and time again to provide mediocre results. Hence why new sales methods come out just about every other year. Companies need to realize that every company that they are selling to has its own personality. That personality will determine how you sell to them. They may be a transactional company, or they could be reactionary. Some only needing or wanting salespeople to answer the phone call or email with a quote. Others want to have the ability to have an order fulfilled when they need or want something. Still others may be looking for its vendor to be a trusted advisor. Looking to them to be an extension of their company and providing them with solutions that fit what they need not what the sales team wants to sell. Use common sense and really listen to your customer.

When you finally embrace a few of the most important things in the sales process, you will succeed. Make sure though of all the information discussed in this book you take one thing above all else, listen. You will find that this will get you further down the path of successful sales than any other. Listen, be humble and you'll have a long career.

All that being said, no matter how good you are, no matter how much you sell, no matter how much your customers love you, you are replaceable. Your fault, my fault, nobody's fault, you can be replaced. It might be due to the company missing numbers, it might be due to overlap from an acquisition, but there is always a chance as a salesperson that you will be looking for work next quarter. Always be prepared and never relax. When you think you have it made is usually when the ax drops.

Make no mistake. Sales is a cutthroat business. It's not for everyone. You can just as easily lose your job as stub your toe, but because of that there will always be a need for good salespeople. The top salespeople are basically hired guns, they come in, do the job, get paid, and you move on. Sounds a little old West. It's not, it's the world that has been created for salespeople so make the most of it!

That's it, that's the end. Thank you for reading! Hopefully this was both educational and mildly entertaining for you! Sales can be a great career if you manage your way through the corporate jungle with common sense!

http://www.iaosynergistics.com/thesalesmanual

www.ingramcontent.com/pod-product-compliance
Lightning Source LLC
Chambersburg PA
CBHW070156230526
4547ICB00002B/689